The Total
Tote Bag Book

The Total Tote Bag Book

Designer Totes to Craft and Carry

by Joyce Aiken and Jean Ray Laury

Taplinger Publishing Company   New York

By Joyce Aiken and Jean Ray Laury

CREATING BODY COVERINGS

HANDMADE RUGS FROM PRACTICALLY ANYTHING

By Jean Ray Laury

NEW USES FOR OLD LACES

WOOD APPLIQUÉ

DOLL MAKING

QUILTS AND COVERLETS

APPLIQUÉ AND STITCHERY

By Jean Ray Laury and Ruth Law

HANDMADE TOYS AND GAMES

■   ■   ■   ■

SECOND PRINTING

Published in the United States in 1977 by
TAPLINGER PUBLISHING CO., INC.
New York, New York

Published simultaneously in the Dominion of Canada by
Burns & MacEachern Limited, Ontario

Library of Congress Cataloging in Publication Data

Aiken, Joyce.
        The total tote bag book.

        1. Tote bags. I. Laury, Jean Ray, joint author. II. Title.
TT667.A35   1977   646.4'8   76-11058

ISBN 0-8008-7793-4 (CLOTH)   ISBN 0-8008-7794-2 (PAPER)

All work in this book is by the authors, except where other
designers are credited.
All drawings and illustrations are the work of the authors.

Designed by Mollie M. Torras

Acknowledgments

We wish especially to thank the many designers who contributed their work: Kay Aronson, Betty Auchard, Carole Austin, Karen Bray, Carole Clark, Sas Colby, Ann de Witt, Lewis de Witt, Robbie Fanning, Gail Giberson, Doris Hoover, Wanda Hottle, Jody House, Vicki Johnson, Marilyn Judson, Bucky King, Mark D. Law, Joan Lewis, Gloria McNutt, Monica Malone, Carole Martin, Peggy Moulton, Carol Olson, Bev O'Neal, Janice Rosenberg, Bea Slater, Gayle Smalley,. and Eleanor Van De Water.

And thanks also to Janice Rosenberg and Bea Slater for their help in sewing, to Gayle Smalley and Stan Bitters for photography, and to Jim Heitzeberg for his help in printing the photographs.

We are particularly appreciative of Terry Taplinger, whose ideas and enthusiasm prompted this book, and Bobs Pinkerton, who so capably and patiently edited our work. Their support and humor added greatly to an already enjoyable collaboration.

Contents

INTRODUCTION   11

1. SHOPPING TOTES   15

2. DAY TOTES   20

3. BUSINESS AND OFFICE TOTES   26

4. TOTES FOR CHILDREN   38

5. HOME AND GARDEN TOTES   49

6. PICNIC AND LUNCH TOTES   56

7. TRAVEL TOTES   66

8. RAINPROOF TOTES   76

9. SEWING TOTES   82

10. SPORT TOTES   88

11. DUFFELS AND SLEEPING BAG CARRIERS   100

12. EVENING TOTES   105

13. A GALLERY OF UNUSUAL TOTES   112

14. THE BASIC TOTES   122

15. FINISHING   146

Handles   146   •   Pockets   151   •   Binding   154
•   Grommeting   155   •   Lettering and Graphics   155   •
Decorating   157

TOTES MADE FROM THE TWELVE BASIC TOTES   158

Illustrations in Color

FACING PAGE

32	Giant totes
32	Trapunto landscape tote
32	Tree bag
33	Striped tie tote
33	Window tote
33	Designer's tote
64	Rat Pak
64	Doll shoulder bag
64	Garden tote
65	Picnic tote
65	Recycled denim tote
65	Plaid picnic tote
96	Travel set
96	All-day bag and shaving kit
96	Pill tote
97	Runaway totes
97	Padded sewing tote
97	Tennis tote
128	To the beach
128	Labeled Levi's
128	Security bag
129	Sleeping bag totes
129	A collection of totes for various uses

Introduction

Totes have been in use since woman first collected nuts and devised a means to bring them home to the cave. The need for them has been universal and the solutions for that need are richly varied. Totes carried seeds, shells, charms, and medicines for the American Plains Indians; coconuts, roots, and fruits for the islanders of the South Pacific. The men who traveled with Marco Polo carried their valuables in totes and the Crusaders had small belted totes for precious bone needles.

Today, totes have come into their own again as they fit so well in contemporary life. And the more varied one's activities and pursuits, the greater the need for a variety of totes. The businesswoman, the homemaker, the teacher, the athlete, or sports buff, vacationers or hobbyists, all have special requirements and equipment. So here is an abundant array of totes—more than a hundred—to meet almost every conceivable need, along with a few which might never actually be *needed*, but would certainly be enjoyed. In short, here is a total tote book.

While we have grouped these totes according to specific use—picnic totes, sewing totes, totes for children, sport totes, totes for rainy weather— almost all of these carriers are made from just twelve, easy, basic patterns. In Chapter 14 we give detailed instructions for these dozen master patterns. And for each individual tote we tell precisely how to vary the basic pattern to make the particular tote shown. In the very few cases when a tote has a unique construction, we give the patterns and special directions.

Chapter 15 includes all the many techniques for pockets, handles, and straps, and for finishing. It is helpful to look at this chapter when you are in the planning stage of a tote and before you cut your material.

Chapter 13, "A Gallery of Unusual Totes," is a collection of highly personal totes made by fiber artists and designers. Some are fantastic, some are humorous, and some display virtuoso needlework and weaving tech-

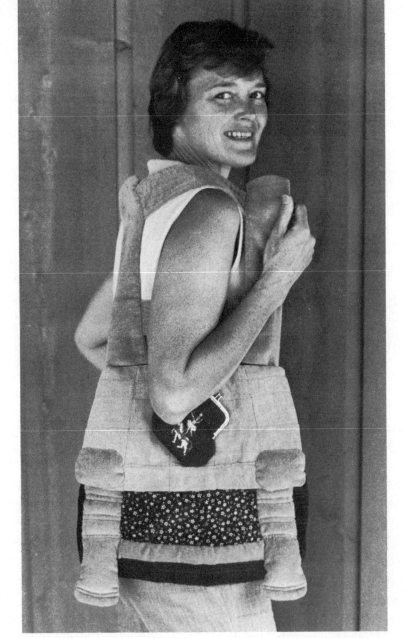

Ann de Witt's chairperson tote is enormous fun, and practical, too.

niques, but all have stimulating ideas. Many of the totes in this book have designs or decorative motifs which you will find applicable to other patterns of totes that better fit your requirements. Fabrics, interior pockets, measurements, and decorations can all be switched around so that you can make yourself an individualized tote. The tote on page 37, for instance, has a

Vicki Johnson combined hand-dyed fabrics and Seminole patchwork
in this efficiently compartmented sewing tote.

changeable, see-through pocket which can be used on almost any tote in this book.

The fabrics are inexpensive and the sewing is simple, so we hope that with *The Total Tote Bag Book* you can make yourself a wardrobe of totes tailored to fit your particular needs. The patterns given will enable you to duplicate the features of a costly or elegant tote that you have admired. Or to make truly personal totes as gifts.

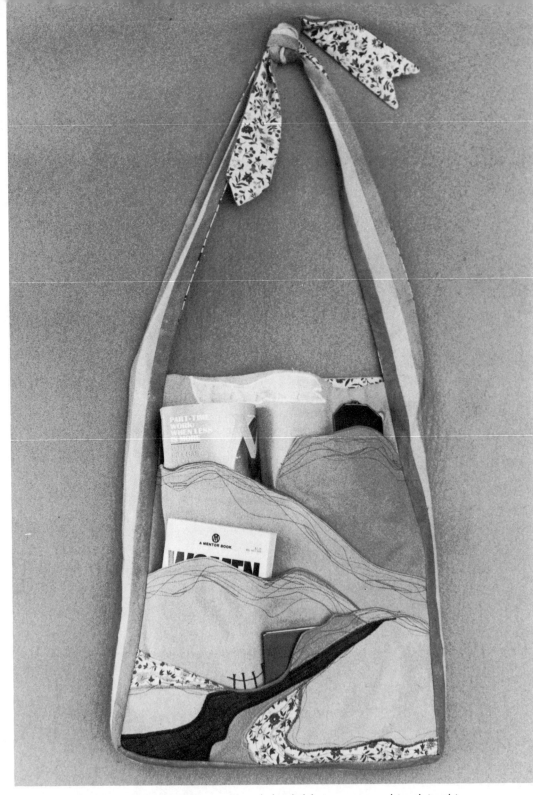

Machine appliqué and embroidery on hand-dyed fabrics are combined in this very personal and very functional bag.

I. Shopping Totes

Few activities make so many demands on totes as shopping. The requirements are fairly simple—shopping totes must be easily carried, comfortable to use, and amply spacious. The construction of the tote, and particularly the attachment of the handle, must be sturdy enough to survive the stress of a heavy load.

The shopping totes that follow are designed to meet a variety of needs. Some simply allow for the morning's errands—picking up film, getting a prescription, buying the dog a new collar, and selecting some yarns for a new project. A tote should willingly accept such a variety. Other totes are made especially for shopping at a farmers' market or the roadside fruit stand where bags are often at a premium. Totes from throughout this book can be used for shopping, most with little or no modification.

Scenic Shopping Tote

Carole Austin designed this bag to help take some of the countryside wherever she goes, even to the supermarket. The landscape on the front of the bag opens so that the top of each of the rolling hills provides a pocket. Here the pockets are used for travel and hold a magazine, paperback, and an address book. It just as readily takes off for the beach, providing spaces for lotions, books, and sunglasses.

The tied handle can be varied in length so that the bag transforms readily from shoulder-length to short handle. The side panels and handle are pieced from three different colored bands of cloth, making a rainbow that surrounds the countryside.

Hand-dyed muslin was used, double thick, to add body to the tote. The appliqué and appliqué stitches add further stiffening. The lining is in a floral pattern.

The grocery list goes with you in this
shopping tote that sports an erasable
plastic panel. By Bea Slater.

16

The finished size is 12½″ (31.8 cm) wide, 15″ (38.1 cm) high, and 2½″ (6.4 cm) deep. This boxed bag is made according to the directions given for Basic Tote #4 (page 128), with the following variations:

1. Cut front and back panels 13½″ wide by 17½″ high (34.3 cm by 44.5 cm).
2. Cut side and bottom panels and handle in one long strip, 3½″ by 96″ (8.9 cm by 243.8 cm). Piece fabric for handles if you want a tricolored band like this one.
3. Finish appliqué before joining parts. Hillsides are double layers of fabric with the top edges finished so they can form pockets.
4. Tie handles together to make shoulder or arm strap.

Shopper's Tote

A piece of clear plastic provides a surface on which to list errands to be run or groceries needed. Here the plastic is backed with white and attached to the flat tote fabric with binding of the printed lining material. Nonpermanent marking pen or wax crayon can be used for writing notes. Both wipe off. Inside pockets provide space for a wiping cloth and the marking pen or crayon. Test pens or crayons on a sample piece of plastic to be sure you use an erasable combination.

Made according to Basic Tote #4 (page 128), this one has an ample over-the-shoulder strap. A bright print was used to line strap and bag and edge the piece of plastic. The finished size is 14″ (35.6 cm) wide, 18″ (45.7 cm) high, and 2½″ (6.4 cm) deep. The strap is 39″ (99.1 cm), top edge to top edge.

Follow the directions for Basic Tote #4, with the following variations:

1. Cut front and back pieces 15″ by 20″ (38.1 cm by 50.8 cm).
2. Cut side and bottom panel 3½″ by 54″ (8.9 cm by 137.2 cm).
3. Cut strap 3″ by 53″ (7.6 cm by 134.6 cm).
4. Cut plastic 14″ by 12″ (35.6 cm by 30.5 cm). Attach to tote while fabric is flat.
5. Attach straps to outside of tote, overlapping strap 6″ (15.2 cm) onto side panels. Topstitch through tote and lining.
6. Add pockets where you wish, following the directions on page 151.

A ready-made bag, with handle added, carries wet clothes from the laundry or beach and it stretches readily to carry melons from the market or garden.

Onion Bag

A bit of imagination and a few minutes transform any ready-made bag into a tote. This onion bag required only the addition of a handle. Designer Peggy Moulton states that it has the additional advantage of being disposable, though it is so lightweight that it can readily be rolled into a tiny package after use.

The openwork weave makes it excellent for carrying fresh produce from the fruit stand or greengrocers. It also offers an advantage for carrying damp or wet articles as the air will circulate.

The fifty-pound onion bag used here is tied with string at each of the bottom corners. It shapes the bag in the same way that boxing the bottom seam does in Basic Tote #2. A second bag is used to provide fabric for a 36″ (91.4-cm) handle, folded over several times for additional strength.

To make a similar bag from mesh fabric, use Basic Tote #2 (page 124) and eliminate the boxing, or use Basic Tote #5 (page 130).

Scarf Tote

A rectangular scarf, already edged or hemmed, provides an almost instant bag. Just two sewn seams and no cutting complete the bag. Basic

Folded, this ready-made scarf tote can be tucked into a pocket—then tied at the top when it is put to use. By Ann de Witt.

Red, white, and blue tote by Ann de Witt. 13″ by 25″ (33 cm by 63.5 cm).

Tote #10, Variation A (page 139) was used to make this top-tied tote in a matter of minutes. When not in use, this tote folds up to something about the size of a handkerchief.

Stars and Stripes

Stars of various sizes are combined with stripes in this boldly patterned bag. The center section is padded and quilted before it is joined to the side panels.

This tote is made from recycled fabric—actually, bunting material.

Follow the directions for Basic Tote #8 (page 136). The measurements are the same.

Giant Striped Tote

This commodious tote will carry an unbelievable number of parcels and packages. Use it for weekend packing, erranding, or for the baby's needs. Since it folds up flat to take almost no room at all, it's great to take traveling. Take it out of the suitcase and use it to pack up all those last-minute purchases. It will fit (unless *over*stuffed) under your seat on the plane.

This is a one-pieced boxed tote. Make it according to directions for Basic Tote #2 (page 124), with the exception of the handles. The finished size is 16″ (40 cm) wide, 13½″ (34.3 cm) high, and 5″ (12.7 cm) deep. Finished handle is 1″ by 22″ (2.5 cm by 55.9 cm). Vary the basic pattern as follows:

1. Cut handles 3″ by 24″ (7.6 cm by 61 cm).
2. Attach on inside of tote with handle extending 1″ (2.5 cm) down from top edge. Here, stripes are matched so handles appear to be continuous.

An entire day's errands can be accomplished and go into this one voluminous tote.

2. Day Totes

This collection of day totes includes an array of casual, serviceable, multi-purpose bags. While they might be carried for any of a variety of reasons, their functions are not specific. They are everyday, all-day, any-day totes.

Flower Tote

Sailcloth was used in the construction of this sturdy all-purpose bag. Rows of top stitching give the handles firmness so that even heavy items can be carried with ease. The boxed bottom helps keep the bag in an upright stance.

The finished bag is 14″ (35.6 cm) wide and 11½″ (29.2 cm) high, with 13″ (33-cm) handles. It is spacious enough for a thermos and brown-bag lunch or for carrying the extra shoes to change to during the day.

Decorative flowers with stuffed, pouchy centers are appliquéd to the front of the bag and the print of the appliqué is repeated in the lining. Designer Karen Bray has added a row of piping to the top edge, but that is optional.

Make according to Basic Tote #2 (page 124), with the following variations:

1. Adjust basic pattern to a cut size of 20″ by 34½″ (50.8 cm by 87.5 cm).
2. Adjust cut size of handle pattern piece to 4″ by 17″ (10.2 cm by 43.2 cm).

Patchwork Poke

Jody House's patchwork poke is made up from a pieced patchwork panel in velvets and cottons. The large section which forms the front and back panels of the tote was cut, patched, and embroidered while flat. Then the patchwork panel was joined to the side pieces.

Appliqué and embroidery highlight the flowers on this blue tote.

Bright patchwork pieces and decorative embroidery make a lively pattern.

The finished size of this tote is 11½″ (29.2 cm) wide and 13″ (33 cm) high. Follow directions for Basic Tote #1 (page 122), with the following variations:

1. Cut basic pattern 12½″ by 32″ (31.8 cm by 81.3 cm).
2. Cut sides 4″ by 15″ (10.2 cm by 38.1 cm).
3. Cut handles 3″ by 15″ (7.6 cm by 38.1 cm).

Printed upholstery-weight material provided a pattern for the decorative trapunto. By Carole Clark.

Trapunto Landscape Tote

This versatile tote of upholstery-weight material is commodious enough to carry numerous bundles. To do a trapunto design like this, select an appropriately patterned fabric and cut the main tote pieces. While the material is still flat, place a second layer of fabric (muslin or similar material) under it. The printed designs can then be outlined with straight machine stitching. When stitching is complete, make small slits in the muslin so that batting can be stuffed in to pad some areas.

A synthetic batting is used for stuffing, and after an area is stuffed, the muslin is slip-stitched shut. All trapunto must be finished while the fabric pieces are lying flat. The completed trapunto sections are then joined as in the basic tote directions and the handle is added. The tote is lined so that the muslin is not exposed.

The finished size of this tote is 15″ by 15″ (38.1 cm by 38.1 cm). Follow directions for Basic Tote #2 (page 124), with the following variations:

1. Cut large pattern piece 21″ by 39″ (53.3 cm by 99.1 cm).
2. Cut handle 20″ by 5″ (50.8 cm by 12.7 cm).
3. After corners are stitched at bottom of bag, add a line of top stitching from base to top, 2½″ (6.4 cm) from each side seam. This adds a crisp look.

A detail of the landscape tote.

Padding is incorporated with machine appliqué in this smart, two-colored tote by Carole Clark.

Tree Bag

The machine-appliquéd oak tree spreads out over the two colors of this shoulder bag. As the appliqué shapes are sewn, batting is stuffed inside to give a raised, three-dimensional surface.

This tote is made according to the directions for Basic Tote #8 (page 136). If you decide to appliqué the front, it is easier to add the side pieces to the front of the bag only. Then the material will be flat so you can easily appliqué. When the appliqué is completed, join to the back.

Denim Heart Bag

Ever-popular denim fabric makes this tote a favorite. The decorative designs are accomplished through the use of trapunto, using both cording and padding. The front section is cut and backed with a piece of lightweight fabric such as muslin. The designs are then outlined in machine stitches. The raised rectangular line is formed by running cording through from the

Plumply stuffed denim heart is
machine-stitched by Carol Olson.

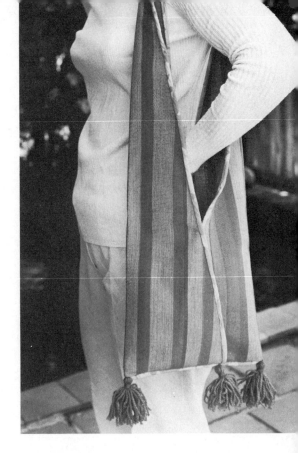

reverse side and threading it between parallel stitched lines. The heart and surrounding circle are stuffed with batting inserted through a small slit made in the backing material. When the decorative work is completed, the front and back sections are joined and lined.

The finished size of this tote is 10″ by 12″ (25.4 cm by 30.5 cm), with a 10″ (25.4-cm) handle. Follow Basic Tote #5 (page 130), with the following variations:

1. Cut pattern pieces, adjusting the cut size of the tote to 11″ (27.9 cm) wide by 15″ (38.1 cm) high.
2. Cut handle 3″ (7.6 cm) wide and 14″ (35.6 cm) long.

Striped Tie Tote

This striped tie tote is simple to make and ingenious in design. The woven stripe offers an interesting variation to the basic pattern. Here cut

Yarn tassels punctuate corners of this simple, handsome tote. Tied over the shoulder, the design makes efficient use of yardage. 27″ (68.6 cm) long. By Ann de Witt.

25

edges were bound with a printed pattern which echoes the colors of the stripes. Yarn tassels were added to the finished bag. Follow directions for Basic Tote #9 (page 138), as this bag is identical in size.

Sunburst Bag

This festively colored bag is highlighted by a cluster of bright wood beads. Bands of needleweaving radiate from the sunlike central motif over cotton velveteen. The needlework was applied to a rectangle of fabric cut according to the basic pattern. The ends of the cords and yarns are secured in the seams that join tote parts.

The strap makes delightful use of wrapping and beading for an over-the-shoulder carrier. The inside of the bag is enriched with a brocade lining, with pockets of various sizes sewn to the lining.

The finished size of the sunburst bag is 12″ (30.5 cm) wide by 9″ (22.9 cm) high, with a 2½″ (6.4-cm) side panel. Follow Basic Tote #4 (page 128), with the following variations:

1. Cut front and back panels 13″ (33 cm) wide, 11½″ (29.2 cm) high.
2. Cut band for sides and bottom 3½″ wide by 33″ (88.9 cm by 83.8 cm).
3. Make strap 36″ (91.4 cm).

Wood beads and detached stitches turn a simple bag into one of special elegance. By Eleanor Van De Water.

3. Business and Office Totes

In Portland, Gallup, Cleveland, or Boston, few toters tote more totes than the women who trek daily to work, school, or office. Every job has its special needs and the tote must meet a variety of specific demands. Often it must be convenient to carry aboard a crowded bus, be large enough to hold the sweater that will be discarded midday, and still be chic enough to carry to a luncheon meeting. The following collection keeps this in mind.

Designer's Tote

Here's a tote that always has room for one more illustration board or one more set of plans. The finished size of this tote is 17″ (43.2 cm) wide by 15½″ (39.4 cm) high, with a strap 2″ by 30″ (5.1 cm by 76.2 cm). It is made according to the directions for Basic Tote #3 (page 126), Variation B (page 128), with the following changes:

1. Cut tote (and lining, optional) 18″ by 18″ (45.7 cm by 45.7 cm).
2. Cut a strap 5″ by 34″ (12.7 cm by 86.4 cm).
3. Add handles to inside of bag.

Giant Office Tote

Upholstery-weight fabric makes a sturdy tote for the office worker who carries paperwork home. This one holds everything. You can even include a miniature version of the same bag. The tiny bag can be brought into action for a dash to the coffee shop or for a luncheon appointment. At the end of the day it is tucked in, like a baby kangaroo in the pouch.

This giant tote is made exactly according to directions for Basic Tote #2 (page 124). The finished size is 16″ (40.6 cm) wide, 13½″ (34.3 cm) high,

and 5″ (12.7 cm) deep. The strap is 1½″ by 9″ (3.8 cm by 22.9 cm). If you
make the accompanying tiny tote, you can do it by the same pattern. Add
pockets according to individual needs, following directions on page 151.

Sketch pads, graph paper, and
architectural drawings fit easily into
a big over-the-shoulder bag.

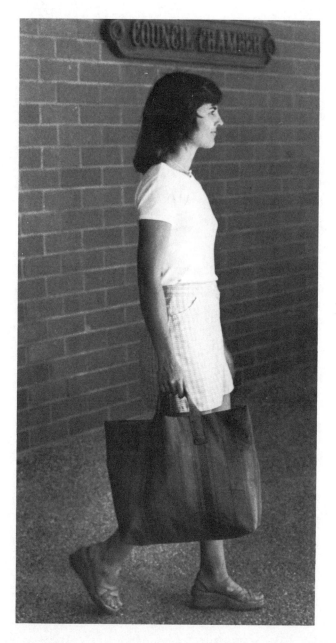

Everything needed at the office goes
into one large bag.
A smaller tote,
suitable for a luncheon date, can be tucked inside
for middle-of-the-day use.

This smart and strong tote goes everywhere—to work, traveling, or shopping.

Canvas Tote

Here's a go-everywhere, do-anything tote. Its tailored simplicity makes it easy to use with many outfits, and because it is stout and hardy, it can survive heavy wear.

The finished size is 15″ (38.1 cm) wide by 18″ (45.7 cm) high, with straps 28″ (71.1 cm) above the top edge. The tote is made according to the directions for Basic Tote #5 (page 130), with the following variations:

1. Cut 2 pieces of colored canvas for trim, 7″ by 16″ (17.8 cm by 40.6 cm).
2. Cut 2 pieces of natural canvas, 16″ by 16″ (40.6 cm by 40.6 cm). ½″ (12-mm) seam allowance included.
3. Sew sides and bottom of tote. Sew 7″ (17.8-cm) ends of trim together. Turn to right sides.
4. Join trim to tote by placing right side of trim inside tote and sewing top edge. Fold trim over itself to outside, hem ½″ (12 mm) and baste in place. Trim will measure 3″ (7.6 cm) above tote.
5. Cut 2 handles 3″ by 42″ (7.6 cm by 106.7 cm). Topstitch.

6. Pin handles to outside of bag, letting handles extend 2½″ (6.4 cm) over the bottom edge of the colored band. Slip brass or silver half rings (from notions department) over ends of straps.
7. Turn strap end under so that end covers ¼″ (6 mm) of top trim. Baste in place.
8. Topstitch handles over colored canvas and topstitch the edge of the colored canvas. Be sure to catch ends of straps in seams.

Monogrammed Tote

Monogramming adds identification as well as a decorative plus. To stencil letters, follow directions on page 155. Here the letters are inked onto a separate tab which is inserted in a seam. This approach is less risky than stenciling directly on the bag. If you make an error on the tab, another one can be cut.

Make this tote according to the directions for the preceding bag, although this tote is smaller.

Stenciled letters are added to a tab which is slipped into the bag seams. 13½″ by 16½″ (34.3 cm by 41.9 cm).

Variations:

1. Cut 2 pieces of colored canvas 6½″ by 14½″ (16.5 cm by 36.8 cm).
2. Cut 2 pieces of natural canvas 14½″ by 14½″ (36.8 cm by 36.8 cm).
3. Cut 2 handles from colored canvas 3″ by 44″ (7.6 cm by 111.8 cm).
4. Cut a tab, 6″ by 6″ (15.2 cm by 15.2 cm), including ½″ (12-mm) seam allowance. Stencil letters on tab and be careful not to print over the seam allowance.
5. Fold tab with right sides facing, and sew each side. Turn. Insert the monogram at the exact center of the side, as in the photograph.
6. Extend straps to bottom of monogram tab, slip on metal rings, and finish as in the previous tote.

Teacher's Tote

The bag was designed by a teacher who carried stacks of books and knew exactly what was needed. Gayle Smalley used a double layer of heavy denim, then ran straps under the bag to help support the books. The handle can fit over the shoulder, but it is not too long to be carried by hand. Legal-size folders fit in nicely.

The finished size is 18″ (45.7 cm) wide by 11″ (27.9 cm) high. Handle is 2″ (5.1 cm) wide. This tote is made according to the directions for Basic Tote #1 (page 122), with the following variations:

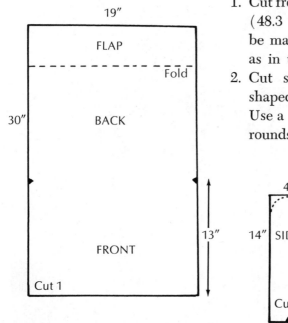

1. Cut front/back panel piece 19″ by 30″ (48.3 cm by 76.2 cm). Notch should be made 13″ (33 cm) from one end as in the diagram.
2. Cut side panels, cutting an arch-shaped flap at the top end of each. Use a saucer to make the arch-shaped rounds.

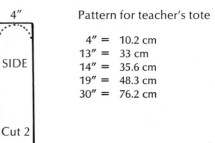

Pattern for teacher's tote

4″ = 10.2 cm
13″ = 33 cm
14″ = 35.6 cm
19″ = 48.3 cm
30″ = 76.2 cm

A double layer of heavy denim makes a strapping, hearty bag
which can carry an armload of books.

3. Cut 4 straps 2″ by 48″ (5.1 cm by 121.9 cm).

4. Use double layer of denim for straps and join ends to make a continuous handle 2″ by 96″ (5.1 cm by 243.8 cm). Sew straps to bag before joining bag to side sections as in the drawing. Place joined ends of handle even with notches. Fringe the edges.

5. Assemble bag according to basic directions except that the seams are on the outside. Cut ends are fringed.

6. Set side panel in so that flap extends above front. Allow back of bag to extend several inches to form a flap.

7. Use a separating zipper if a zipper closing is used (optional).

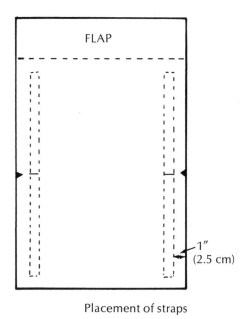

FLAP

1″ (2.5 cm)

Placement of straps

A voluminous tote carries *everything* to the office five days a week, to the beach on Saturday, and to the country on Sunday. By Bea Slater.

Blue Denim 24-Hour Tote

Here's a bag big enough to carry a change of clothes. Doubling as a weekender, it'll accommodate a beach towel and swimsuit. Extra sweater and sneakers easily fit in along with everything else.

The finished size is 16" (40.6 cm) wide, 16" (40.6 cm) high, and 5" (12.7 cm) deep. Handle is 32" (81.3 cm) from one side to the other. It is made according to Basic Tote #2 (page 124), with the following variations:

1. Cut tote piece 22" by 44" (55.9 cm by 111.8 cm).
2. Cut straps 3" by 46" (7.6 cm by 116.8 cm), 1 from tote material, the other from contrasting lining material.
3. Assemble according to directions.
4. Fold over 3" (7.6 cm) of tote material to the inside instead of just 1½" (3.8 cm).
5. Place handles at boxed end.
6. Finish ends of handles, overlap 6" (15.2 cm) onto bag. Topstitch in place.

Black and White Book Tote

A book bag for school, office, or library books keeps them all together and ready to go. The finished size is 14" (35.6 cm) wide by 16" (40.6 cm)

Three giant totes made from the same basic pattern serve the office worker, weekend traveler, or bus-riding shopper.
(Photo by Jean Ray Laury)

print is worked in trapunto to give a
pted effect. By Carole Clark.
oto by Stan Bitters)

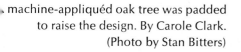
machine-appliquéd oak tree was padded
to raise the design. By Carole Clark.
(Photo by Stan Bitters)

An over-the-shoulder bag by Ann de Witt.
(Photo by Stan Bitters)

This clear plastic window will show off
a scarf or a photograph.
(Photo by Jean Ray Laury)

A capacious tote for a designer or an architect. (Photo by Jean Ray Laur

A library bag keeps your overdue books in one place so the bag can be picked up as you head out the door. Small pocket on inside holds library card and change for fines.

An over-the-shoulder carrier is deep and roomy in quilted fabric.

high. Make this tote according to Basic Tote #1 (page 122), with the following variations:

1. Cut front/back panel 15″ by 34″ (38.1 cm by 86.4 cm).
2. Cut 2 pieces for top band 15″ by 5″ (38.1 cm by 12.7 cm), and sew to ends of front/back panel, right sides together. Fold band over itself to inside and blindstitch to seam. Turn ends in and blindstitch closed.
3. Assemble tote according to basic directions.
4. Handle is cut 3″ by 23″ (7.6 cm by 58.4 cm). Sew, turn, and attach to inside of tote.

Tote-It-Along

A bright quilted fabric adds to the charm of this unusual-shaped bag. It's handy for toting lunch or lecture notes.

The finished size of the tote is 8″ by 15″ (20.3 cm by 38.1 cm), with a 38″ (96.5-cm) handle. Make this tote exactly according to Basic Tote #3, Variation A (page 127).

Artist's Carryall

Upholstery cotton makes up this special carrying case edged in corduroy. Perfect for the graphic artist, architect, or designer, it holds a layout pad 14″ by 17″ (35.6 cm by 43.2 cm) and has pockets sewn in the lining for pens, pencils, and inks. The portfolio serves not only to transport drawing or lettering materials, but also to keep them organized and provide storage.

The finished size of this tote is 21″ (53.3 cm) wide, 18″ (45.7 cm) high, and 4″ (10.2 cm) deep. Follow directions for Basic Tote #2 (page 124), with the following variations:

1. If you plan to make a two-color tote as shown here, cut the print 26″ by 33″ (66 cm by 83.8 cm). Cut corduroy top bands 26″ by 9″ (66 cm by 22.9 cm). Join the corduroy bands to the ends of the print, making rectangle 26″ by 49″ (66 cm by 124.5 cm).
2. Cut lining 26″ by 33″ (66 cm by 83.8 cm). Proceed according to basic directions.
3. Pockets on the lining are sewn while lining is flat. Make divisions according to personal needs. See page 152 for pockets.

Pads, papers, inks, and pens all have their special compartments in this roomy carryall. By Ann de Witt.

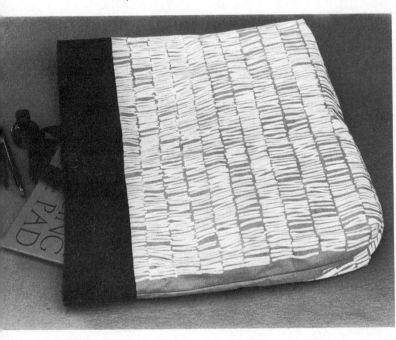

The pockets in the artist's carryall.

An all-silk, over-the-shoulder bag drapes softly and feels elegant.

Leather is stitched, seams out, in this versatile and handsome tote.

4. Slip lining into tote and baste top of lining to tote. Fold corduroy band over itself to inside ½″ (12 mm) and blindstitch to lining.

5. Cut handles 4″ by 16″ (10.2 cm by 40.6 cm). Fold lengthwise in half with right sides together and stitch. Turn. Tuck raw ends under ½″ (12 mm) and blindstitch.

6. Topstitch handles to outside of tote, letting handles overlap the top 4″ (10.2 cm) of bag. This leaves a 7″ (17.8-cm) handle with inside edge of the handles 3½″ (8.9 cm) apart.

Silk Three-Piece Tote

This handsome, solid-colored silk tote will carry papers and notebooks to business lunches and conferences. It is reversible so it can be done in two colors that will go with almost any outfit.

Make it according to directions for Basic Tote #8 (page 136). It is identical in measurement (13″ by 13″ [33 cm by 33 cm]) and finished with a shoulder strap that extends 12″ (30.5 cm) from each side.

Executive's Bag

This simple, straightforward bag in leather is made according to Basic Tote #4 (page 128). The finished size is 10½″ (26.7 cm) high, 9″ (22.9 cm) wide, and 3″ (7.6 cm) deep. Handles are 15″ (38.1 cm) long.

Variations from basic pattern:

1. Cut basic tote pieces 9″ by 10½″ (22.9 cm by 26.7 cm).
2. Cut side and bottom panels separately rather than in a single strip. Cut size for sides 3″ by 12″ (7.6 cm by 30.5 cm). Cut size for bottom 3″ by 9″ (7.6 cm by 22.9 cm).
3. Sew with wrong sides of leather facing so seams will be on the outside. Stitch evenly since top stitching will show.
4. Cut leather strips 1¾″ by 15″ (4.4 cm by 38.1 cm). With wrong sides together, stitch on long edges to within 2″ (5.1 cm) of each end.
5. Turn under top edge of side pieces and glue down with leather glue.
6. Open ends of handles, overlapping 1½″ (3.8 cm) onto bag, and glue or stitch.

Office Tote

The office tote is easy to carry, even when it is loaded down with correspondence, books, or a weekend's packing. It is the twin sister of the artist's carryall (page 34), and is made in the same way, except as follows:

1. Add snaps, grippers, or Velcro fasteners to the top border of the tote on the outside. Fold top corners toward the inside center of bag to determine desired shape. This one has snaps added 2″ (5.1 cm) down from the top and 6″ (15.2 cm) in from the side seam on each side.

A magnificently spacious tote can take all the desk work home for the weekend. 20″ (50.8 cm) at base, 7″ (17.8 cm) at top, by 18″ (45.7 cm) high. By Ann de Witt.

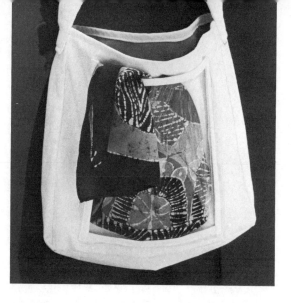

Window Tote

A clear, flexible plastic panel on a white bag makes it possible for this tote to match anything. The window is open at the top so that a light cardboard, covered with fabric to match a blouse or a dress, can be inserted. A scarf, favorite photograph, cartoons, or a calendar work equally well.

The finished size of this bag is 12½″ (31.8 cm) wide by 13″ (33 cm) high. The finished handle is 2½″ by 18½″ (6.4 cm by 47 cm). Make according to Basic Tote #4 (page 128), with the following variations:

1. Cut tote material according to pattern.
2. Cut a piece of clear, flexible plastic or acetate 9½″ by 11″ (22.9 cm by 27.9 cm). Plastic is available in some fabric shops, dime stores, etc. It is sold by the yard in several weights. Use a middle or heavy weight.
3. Bind top edge of the plastic with a strip of the tote fabric cut about 1″ (2.5 cm) wide, turning under raw edges. Use large stitches to avoid cutting plastic.
4. Cut binding for the other three edges. Sew one edge of binding to plastic. Turn and topstitch other edge to tote front as in the drawing.
5. Assemble bag according to directions.
6. Cut fabric for handle 6″ by 19½″ (15.2 cm by 49.5 cm). Make according to directions (page 146) and attach to side panels of bag, overlapping on outside of bag by 1½″ (3.8 cm).

Binding the acetate window

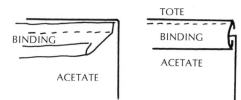

4. Totes for Children

Children are notorious for (among other things) misplacing, forgetting, discarding, and otherwise losing everything from their bike-lock keys and bite plates to their shoes and sweaters. Make totes special, and if they don't lose the tote, they'll keep track of all their possessions. So try to alleviate the sorrow of losses by providing a convenient way of keeping treasures intact.

Tamelin's Stuff

This delightful tote includes an assortment of surprises for a young girl. Gloria McNutt has skillfully combined trapunto, quilting, and appliqué in this soft, bulky bag for her daughter. Tamelin's stuff fits into the numerous recesses and pockets of this hopsack creation.

The finished size is 11″ by 12″ (27.9 cm by 30.5 cm), with a 30″ (76.2-cm) handle. Follow directions for Basic Tote #1 (page 122). Parts are assembled according to the pattern.

Variations:

1. The basic shape is cut 13″ by 38″ (33 cm by 96.5 cm) which includes seam allowance and flap. Cut for tote and lining.
2. Side sections are cut 3½″ by 12½″ (8.9 cm by 31.8 cm). Cut for tote and lining.
3. The strap is cut the same width as the sides and can be made shoulder length (32″ [81.3 cm] on this one) or short.
4. This bag has appliqué, trapunto, and quilting added in richly assorted ways. All decorative work and pockets should be applied to the material while it is flat and before parts are assembled.

This tote is a little girl's dream.
Identified by name in bright appliqué,
it is carried over the shoulder.

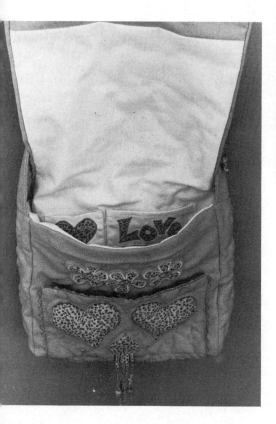

Pockets on the inside of
Tamelin's stuff.

If there are children in the house, there is probably an oatmeal box—and there are probably small toys strewn about. Here the two get together.

Oatmeal Box Tote

A cardboard cylinder provides a perfect tote base. Here, quilted fabric is combined with another print to make a completely lined toy carrier.

This tote is made exactly according to directions for Basic Tote #7 (page 134). The diameter of the box is 5½″ (14 cm), and the tote is 16″ (40.6 cm) high.

Lesson Tote

Several fabric cylinders are clustered to make this unusual tote. It provides pockets for objects of all sizes and shapes. This lesson bag can be varied and adapted to fit the needs of anyone taking a special class. Leotards and dancing slippers could fit into one section, with pockets for keys, spending money, comb, or snacks.

Here the bag contains recorders and music. Since recorder musicians often change instruments during a performance, this tote offers a means of holding the instruments so that they need not be put on the floor.

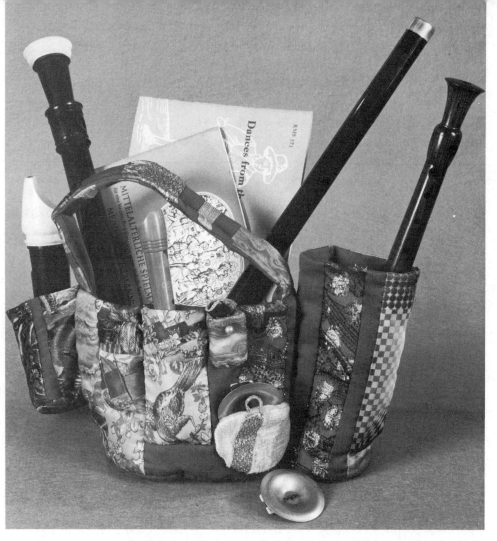

Brilliantly patterned, stuffed patchwork cylinders combine to form
a cluster of convenient pockets.

Vicki Johnson has made these cylinders from pieced and patched
fabrics in a dazzling array of prints and patterns. Some of the little pockets
button shut while others remain ready to accept additional gear. There are
seven cylinders in all and several are lidded. Tiny pockets complete the tote.

To make this tote, construct the individual cylinders according to the
directions for Basic Tote #7 (page 134). Vary the size of the cylinders as
needed, and stuff or quilt them for a soft, padded effect. The main cylinder
here is 5½″ (14 cm) tall. There is a 12″ (30.5-cm) handle. The cylinders
are whipstitched together.

This drawstring pouch holds no end of treasure for the young collector of sticks and stones, shells and bones.

Kid's Carryall

A drawstring tote, slipped over the wrist or tied to a belt, will keep a variety of essentials ready for any child. Bike keys and lunch money could find room among the wild assortment that usually fills a youngster's pockets. Add initials, name, address, iron-on appliqué, or message to identify the bag (see pages 155-157).

This tote is made exactly according to directions in Basic Tote #6 (page 131). The finished size is 10″ (25.4 cm) wide by 12″ (30.5 cm) high. The cord is 36″ (91.4 cm) long.

Stocking Cap Tote

A recycled stocking cap becomes a tote to be carried to any sporting event. The skier will find it handy to hold locker key and lip ice, and the football enthusiast can tie it to a belt to leave both hands free for cheering.

A tie-on tote is fashioned
from a discarded stocking cap
by Doris Hoover.

A boy's special tote carries his
white rat, leaving his hands free to
ride his bike. By Carole Austin.

The stocking cap is used so that the folded end provides a channel for the drawstring. The other end is embellished with yarns and tassels. Braided yarns with beads knotted at the ends make matching ties.

To sew the drawstring channel, see directions in Basic Tote #6 (page 131). The finished size is 6" by 12" (15.2 cm by 30.5 cm).

Rat Pak

The rat pak may be an unusual tote, but certainly one that many young animal lovers will welcome. The designer made this bag for her son who found it difficult to carry his white rat while riding his bike.

The shoulder strap slips over his head so that the pak fits smoothly against his side. The white rat (or mouse, hamster, or gerbil) enters through the zipper door. The buttonhole-stitched circle at the bottom allows the animal to stick his nose out to sniff the air. The air hole has a plastic ring stitched in.

The rat pak is not meant to provide protection over any long period of time. But it does provide a safe, easy way to transport a very small pet for a short distance, leaving the cyclist with both hands on the handlebars.

The finished size of this tote is 7" by 9" (17.8 cm by 22.9 cm), with a 29" (73.7 cm) strap.

The rat pak is sewn essentially like Basic Tote #5 (page 130), with some obvious changes. To make a similar tote:

1. Cut 2 rectangles of sturdy fabric 8″ by 10″ (20.3 cm by 25.4 cm) (includes seam allowance).
2. In one side, set a 7″ (17.8-cm) or 8″ (20.3-cm) zipper. Add buttonholed plastic ring, embroidery, and machine appliqué.
3. Cut strip of fabric 31″ by 3″ (78.7 cm by 7.6 cm). Join long edges with a ½″ (12-mm) seam. Turn and press.
4. Open zipper. Pin handle to one of the tote pieces. Then, right sides together, pin and baste front of tote to back, catching strap in basting line. Sew all four sides.
5. Turn through zipper openings.

Toy Tote

Zippers sewn to a yard square of fabric form a carryall bag for objects of any size or shape. This tote, made according to Basic Tote #10 (page

Here toys are tucked into the tote which, unzipped, provides a play pad. By Eleanor Van De Water.

139), Variation C (page 141), can be carried by the pointed ends, or the ends can be tied to make a handle. This arrangement is great for carrying toys, since the bag itself opens up to provide a play area. When it is time to go home, toys are tossed onto the fabric, it's zippered up, and away they go!

Walrus Tote

An absurd walrus lounges over the front of a tote made from corded fabric. Lining is of a related plaid cotton. The pattern consists of just two identical triangles. To add appliqué, the overlapping triangles are sewn on one side only. Then when the appliqué is completed, the second side and bottom seams can be sewn. A silk-screened walrus was printed by Lewis de Witt on white fabric, cut out, and used for the appliqué.

To make this bag, follow directions and sizes for Basic Tote #9 (page 138). The measurements are identical.

Walrus tote ties over the shoulder. By Ann de Witt.

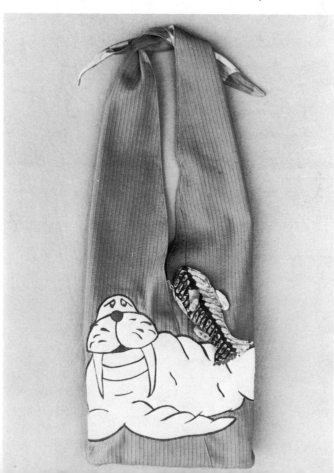

Doll Shoulder Bag

An irresistible bag in the form of a companion clasps its fabric hands to hang over a child's shoulder. The body is made in a basic bag form with a long sleeved T-shirt pulled over the top. Arms and legs are stuffed and inserted in the seams. A flap, added to one side of the bag, folds over the top and provides the panel for the appliqué of a beaming face.

Inside this bag a whole new world of activities is stored. Pockets, games, secret compartments, and crayons provide entertainment for any youngster, and is especially helpful for the young traveler. Here's back-seat enjoyment to last from Los Angeles to Boston.

Two identical pieces form the front and back panels, with a side inset panel as shown in Basic Tote #4 (page 128). The flap, an extension of the back, forms the appliquéd face.

The finished size of the tote is 16″ (40.6 cm) wide by 37″ (94 cm) high (from fingertips to end of toe) or 14″ (35.6 cm) high, measuring just the body of the bag.

Refer to Basic Tote #4 but follow these variations:

1. Cut the pattern parts. Cut 1 side and bottom panel 4″ by 40″ (10.2 cm by 101.6 cm). Lining is needed for front and back panels and for side and bottom panel.
2. Appliqué the features to one of the flaps. Use either machine appliqué (as is used here) or hand stitching. Appliqué bias tape for tic-tac-toe on the second flap.

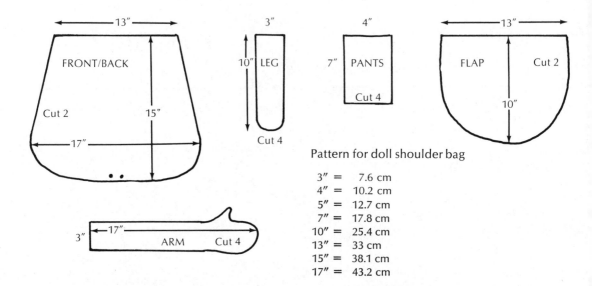

Pattern for doll shoulder bag

3″ =	7.6 cm
4″ =	10.2 cm
5″ =	12.7 cm
7″ =	17.8 cm
10″ =	25.4 cm
13″ =	33 cm
15″ =	38.1 cm
17″ =	43.2 cm

Here's a fabric bag, full of surprises and almost as big as the child for whom it was made. By Gloria McNutt.

Pockets and tic-tac-toe inside shoulder bag.

3. Place flaps with right sides facing and pin. Add padding, cut the same size. (Use a blanket, cotton flannel, or any other padding that will not shift.) Baste all 3 layers together and stitch. Turn right side out.

4. Make a series of pockets and sew them to both tote and lining parts. Follow the pocket suggestions in the photograph or plan yours to meet personal preferences.

5. Make legs by joining 2 fabric pieces, right sides facing, at sides and bottom. Turn right side out. Stuff with Dacron or polyester batting. Then stitch across center to make a jointed knee. Turn under and hem ¼″ (6 mm) on bottom of pants parts. Then join side seams to make 2 pant legs.

Detail of appliquéd features

Stitching across leg to form a jointed knee

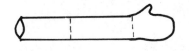

6. Slide legs inside pants and baste top raw ends together. Use doll shoes, baby shoes, or make felt shoes and tie or stitch them to the ends of the legs.

7. Join arms, right sides facing. Baste and sew, then clip and turn. Stuff with batting. Topstitch at elbow and wrist to make a flexible joint.

8. Using a child's T-shirt, cut off the long sleeves and slide them over the stuffed arms to determine size needed. Cut so they fit to the wrists, then take side seams in to make sleeves fit. Baste raw ends of sleeves to raw ends of arms.

9. Join tote front to side inset panel as described in basic directions. Add extra padding by cutting it the same size as tote parts. Catch it in seams that join tote front to side panel and side to back. Also baste legs in place between tote front and the inset panel. Legs are 1″ (2.5 cm) apart, with inside of each leg meeting the dot on the tote pattern.

10. Join back and front lining pieces to the side inset lining. Slip lining into tote.

11. Slide body of the child's T-shirt over the tote, using the hemmed lower edge of shirt so that it comes down to about 5″ (12.7 cm) above seam at lower tote front. Make shirt smaller, if necessary, so it fits easily but snugly over the body of the bag. Cut top off to meet top raw edge of tote.

12. Flip T-shirt material to inside of tote so that right side of T-shirt faces lining. Pin raw edges together at top.

13. Place flap (with appliqué face) between the T-shirt and the back of tote. Top edge should be basted to top raw edge of tote. The face should be turned so that it faces the front of the tote on the inside.

14. Insert arms between tote and T-shirt seam so that arms match side inset panel.

15. Check pins and basting to be sure all parts are correctly positioned. Then machine-stitch, taking 2 lines of stitching, ¼″ (6 mm) and ½″ (12 mm) from raw edge. Bind raw edge (optional).

16. Turn right side out so T-shirt covers body and face serves as flap over front of tote.

17. Join arms of bag by overlapping the hands to make over-the-shoulder strap. Several tacking stitches should go all the way through both hands. Then whipstitch at edge.

5. Home and Garden Totes

Everyday chores become special tasks when there are colorful, useful totes to assist. They keep materials located and organized, avoiding any last-minute dash for the requisite tools, or a search for the proper equipment.

Add a little flair to your jaunt to the Laundromat by carrying a morale-boosting, cheerfully colored tote. Whether you're harvesting from your garden or tending houseplants, a tote will be helpful and pleasant to use.

Zippered Gardener's Tote

Anyone who has gone out to pick the zucchini or the radishes knows that the gardener never makes it all the way back to the kitchen door without a tote to carry the harvest. Here is an unusual one.

This simply made tote is expansive, and when not in use it folds up into a square no larger than a folded scarf. By Eleanor Van De Water.

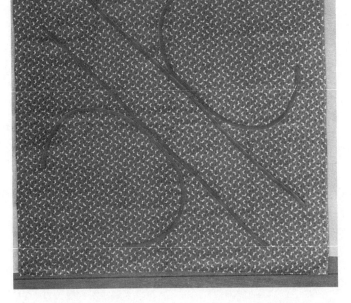

A single square of fabric, with zippers sewn to the surface, transforms itself into a tote. It lies out flat to receive its contents, then zips up and ties at the top to form a handle. Openings at the side offer access to the interior. When vegetables or fruits, whether from the garden or farmers' market, are carried indoors, the fabric is unzipped and no extra handling of the produce is required.

The filled bag is about 18″ (45.7 cm) across, 6″ (15.2 cm) deep, and about 15″ (38.1 cm) to the knot. Make exactly according to Basic Tote #10, following directions for Variation B (page 140).

Garden Tote

The garden tote has ample room for tools and materials, whether the garden is windowbox size or backyard size. A cardboard carton from the grocery store was covered with cotton fabrics. When finished, the underneath bottom and sides were spraycoated with acrylic sealer. While this is not essential, it will help prevent any moisture from softening the cardboard.

The finished size of this box is 11″ by 16″ (27.9 cm by 40.6 cm), with a 3″ (7.6-cm) depth. Each handle is 24″ (61 cm) from top of one side to top of the other.

Follow instructions for Basic Tote #12 (page 143), except for the following variations:

Hand tools, seeds, and plant food all fit easily into a single container in which they can be carried or stored.

1. Cut handles 43″ by 2½″ (109.2 cm by 6.3 cm) and attach by bringing the ends together on the underside of box. Glue handles across bottom of box with fabric glue.
2. Add envelope-like pockets at each end, sewn to the stitched seam allowance of the outside tote fabric.

Gardener's Tote

Botanical prints on the fabric were cut and appliquéd with top stitching to a matched apron and tote. On the tote, the top finished edge of the print is left open to form a large pocket.

The finished size of this bag is 11″ (27.9 cm) wide by 12″ (30.5 cm) high. Handles are 1″ by 15″ (2.5 cm by 38.1 cm). Follow instructions for Basic Tote #1 (page 122), with the following variations:

1. Cut rectangle 12½″ by 32″ (31.8 cm by 81.3 cm). Cut sides 5″ by 18″ (12.7 cm by 45.7 cm). Cut handles 3″ by 18″ (7.6 cm by 45.7 cm).
2. Cut front pocket and pocket lining 12″ by 13″ (30.5 cm by 33 cm). Cut side pocket 5″ by 7″ (12.7 cm by 17.9 cm).

Matching tote and apron
are for the woman with
a bright green thumb.

3. Turn top and bottom of side pocket under ¼″ (6 mm) and hem by top-stitching. With right sides together, sew front pocket and pocket lining on all sides, leaving a 4″ (10.2-cm) opening on one side to turn. Turn and blindstitch closed.

4. Topstitch large pocket to front and side pocket to side, 6″ (15.2 cm) from top.

5. Assemble as in basic instructions. The handles are attached to inside of tote.

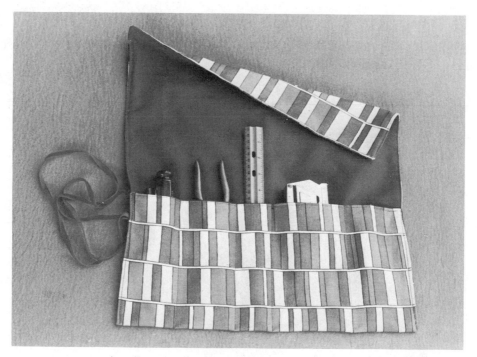

Handy roll-up tool kit keeps all the essentials at fingertip. Finished size, when folded shut, is 12″ by 18″ (30.5 cm by 45.7 cm).

Ms.'s Tool Kit

For kitchen or car, here's a way to keep your tool collection intact for emergency use. Make this tote according to directions for Basic Tote #11 (page 142). All measurements are identical to those used there.

Gift Bags

These gaily patterned bags have just undergone metamorphosis—from scrap and old-clothes bag to patterned gift bags. Use them to wrap gifts, or make a collection of bags to fit into a larger one—give a bagful of bags! Here, at last, is a gift wrap that won't be discarded. Slip a gift book into one of the tiny totes that can later double as a shoe bag. Or wrap a small gift in a bag that becomes a valuable travel aid.

The finished sizes of these gift totes are 6″ by 9″ (15.2 cm by 22.9 cm) and 7″ by 9″ (17.8 cm by 22.9 cm).

Make these according to Basic Tote #3 (page 126), then add a draw-

Brightly colored scraps are pieced and patched to make easy gift wrappings that don't get thrown away.

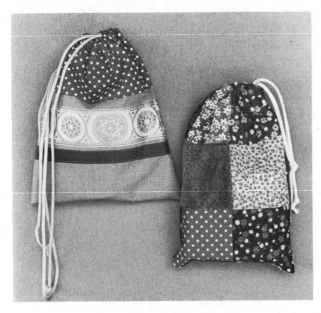

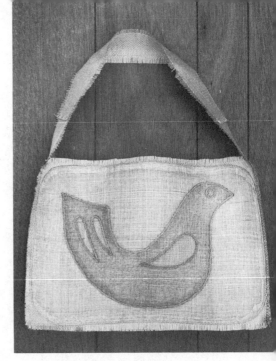

Woven fiber place mats make a lightweight summer, and washable tote. By Eleanor Van De Water.

string top. Or join fabric to make the basic rectangle and use Basic Tote #6 (page 131), except for the following variations:

1. For the larger bag, cut basic rectangle 13″ by 11½″ (33 cm by 29.2 cm).
2. For the smaller tote, cut basic rectangle 11″ by 11″ (27.9 cm by 27.9 cm).

Place Mat Tote

This washable, carry-anything tote is made up from four inexpensive woven mats. The two basic mats, in bright orange, are 13″ by 19″ (33 cm by 48.3 cm). A slightly smaller mat, 12″ by 18″ (30.5 cm by 45.7 cm), oval in shape with a bird decorating it, was sewn to one of the orange mats to make an outside pocket.

The fourth place mat was cut into 4″ (10.2-cm) widths to make the sides and handle. Follow assembly instructions for Basic Tote #4 (page 129). Directions for cutting and seam allowance do not apply since the mats are precut and finished. Seams can be left exposed on the outside of the tote, forming a fiber fringe.

Hobo Tote

This tote is none other than the old bandanna with four corners tied together. By having squares of fabric in several different sizes, a regular wardrobe of hobo bags can be kept on hand. When not serving as totes, they'll double as head scarves.

Objects to be carried can be placed in the center of the flat cloth, then the corners can be pulled up and tied. Four ample openings remain for the removal or addition of other items.

Bev's Tote

Vegetables fill this tote made from a seed bag woven of plastic. It is deep enough to hold a day's picking from the garden, with a finished size of 14″ (35.6 cm) high, 6″ (15.2 cm) wide, and 3½″ (8.9 cm) deep. Handles are 1″ (2.5 cm) wide and 12″ (30.5 cm) above top of tote.

It is made according to the instructions for Basic Tote #2 (page 124), with the following variations:

1. Cut front/back panel 10½″ by 36″ (26.7 cm by 91.4 cm) and handles 3″ by 15″ (7.6 cm by 38.1 cm).
2. Make according to basic directions, sewing a 3½″ (8.9-cm) seam at bottom to box tote.
3. Attach handles to inside of bag.

The corners of a square piece of fabric tie together to make a simple and very practical tote. By Ann de Witt.

Woven plastic fabric makes an ideal tote for harvesting. By Bev O'Neal.

6. Picnic and Lunch Totes

Of all the totes there are to make, few are more fun than those made for picnics or lunches. Perhaps it is the anticipation of the relaxing hour of visiting, or sitting outdoors, and, of course, of eating.

Picnic Tote

An old-fashioned bushel basket is decked out for an old-fashioned picnic. It's amply sized to carry food for a whole family or the whole office staff. The basic assembly is similar to that of the cylinders in Basic Tote #7 (page 134). The top of the bag is drawn to outside of basket. A drawstring is run through to keep the cover in place. When the drawstring is untied, the cover can be removed for washing.

Measure the base of your basket as well as the distance around on the inside near the bottom and near the top. Openings will be needed to allow handles to come through. Inside pockets hold tablecloth, napkins, utensils, bottles, thermos, etc. This picnic tote is sewn in a variety of red and white fabrics including prints, checks, ginghams, and polka dots.

Plaid Picnic Tote

Car picnics are not uncommon for travelers, whether they eat "on the go" or stop by the side of the road. Here a fabric-covered box makes a colorful carrier with room for napkins, paring knife, cups, and food.

This tote is 11″ (27.9 cm) wide, 8″ (20.3 cm) high, and 7″ (17.8 cm) deep, and made according to Basic Tote #12 (page 143). The handles are

This basket holds everything needed for a festive picnic.
The variety of prints give a holiday atmosphere.

A sturdy box will carry the lunch to a convenient stopping place.

held in place with buttons sewn to the outside of the box, 2″ (5.1 cm) from the top edge.

The handles are cut 2″ (5.1 cm) by 88″ (223.5 cm). If two lengths of straps are used, use 44″ (111.8-cm) straps. These handles were made of naugahyde and the edge was folded under to meet at the center back. They are machine-stitched ¼″ (6 mm) from each edge. The seams where the handles are joined are placed under the box.

The Way to My Heart

Access to Carole Martin's heart is obviously through this well-planned picnic tote. It is sewn from cotton duck, and a pocket at one end holds the napkins. Additional pockets on the inside of this bag hold cups and thermos.

The stitched handles are firm and make the bag easy to carry. The letters on this bag are felt-appliquéd with a blind stitch.

Other methods for adding lettering are described beginning on page 155.

The finished size of this tote is 17″ (43.2 cm) wide, 12″ (30.5 cm) high, and 4″ (10.2 cm) deep. The finished handles are 16″ (40.6 cm) long. It is made according to Basic Tote #2 (page 124), with the following variations:

1. Cut tote panel 22″ by 32″ (55.9 cm by 81.3 cm). Cut 2 straps 5″ by 21″ (12.7 cm by 53.3 cm).
2. Add 2 rows of top stitching at the top edge of the tote.

A picnic tote of canvas-weight fabric is lined in bright print which matches the napkins and appliquéd heart.

3. Add 3 rows of top stitching to straps.
4. The appliquéd heart and the felt letters are sewn to the tote fabric before parts are joined.

Lunch Tote

Canvas makes a washable lunch bag. The lime green vinyl lining is removable and attached to the outer bag with Velcro fasteners. The finished bag is 8″ (20.3 cm) wide by 10″ (25.4 cm) high, with a depth of 3″ (7.6 cm).

Make it according to Basic Tote #2 (page 124), with the following variations:

1. Cut tote piece and lining 12″ by 25″ (30.5 cm by 63.5 cm). Cut 2 pieces 3″ by 18″ (7.6 cm by 45.7 cm) for the handle. For handle tabs cut 4 pieces 3″ by 4″ (7.6 cm by 10.2 cm).
2. Finish tabs and handles according to page 146. Rings are slipped on tabs, tab ends turned under, and tabs are topstitched to bag on front and back 2½″ (6.4 cm) apart. Slip handles through rings. Fold up 1″ (2.5 cm) and reinforce.
3. Sew vinyl lining, but do not turn. Sew Velcro fasteners on wrong side of lining and wrong side of bag and slip lining in.

A vinyl-lined canvas tote is large enough for lunch for one or two.

Appliqué and embroidery turn ordinary corduroy into a lunch bag that avoids all possibility of someone mistaking your lunch bag for his or hers. By Karen Bray.

Rainbow Lunch Bag

An embroidered rainbow stretches over this corduroy bag on which appliquéd birds and bead raindrops flourish. Made according to Basic Bag #7 (page 134), this one uses a variation for the drawstring channel. Lining from inside the bag is brought to the outside and is topstitched, going through both layers. The second stitched line of the channel is sewn under the first, so that a drawstring can go through to close the bag. If the tote is not lined, a 3″ (7.6-cm) strip of binding fabric can be used at the top. A ½″ (12-mm) seam joins the band to the inside of the top edge of the tote. The strip is then folded to the outside, raw edge is turned under, and it is topstitched.

A gallon plastic bleach bottle was cut off and used inside this lunch bag. If the bag is lined, the cutoff plastic bottle can be completely covered. Or, line the tote, then insert the plastic bottle (cut from 4″ [10.2 cm] to 6″ [15.2 cm] high) so that the plastic can be removed to be rinsed or sponged out. For the brown bagger who carries an exotic lunch, this rigid form will keep the slice of quiche or the cheesecake from being squashed.

Traveling Coffee Tote

For a coffee connoisseur who prefers to brew her own first cup of the day even away from home, here is a traveling coffee kitchen. This tote is padded and lined, and its dimensions fit perfectly a small percolator, coffee, and accompanying necessities. Such a handsome bag can accompany the

The coffee aficionado will applaud this tote, specially made to carry coffee-making essentials on a trip. By Joan Lewis.

coffee fancier on vacation to motel, hotel, or cottage. The GOOD MORNING on this bag is accomplished with transparent appliqué.

The finished size of the tote is 18″ (45.7 cm) wide, 13″ (33 cm) high, and 4″ (10.2 cm) deep. Make this tote according to Basic Tote #1 (page 122), with the following variations:

1. Cut tote piece 19″ by 32½″ (48.3 cm by 82.6 cm). Cut 2 side panels 5″ by 14½″ (12.7 cm by 36.8 cm). Cut handles 4″ by 18″ (10.2 cm by 45.7 cm).
2. Add all quilting, appliqué, and any other decorative work to flat piece before assembly.
3. Finished handles are placed 6″ (15.2 cm) apart at center of bag on each side.

Bag It

For the office worker who carries lunch, here's a "bag it" bag which is small enough to fit in a larger tote. Designed to hold a small thermos, fruit, and a sandwich perfectly, it can (after lunch) be folded up and tucked away. So many organizations and workshops are now set up on a "bring your own lunch" basis—and here's the bag to take.

The lettering is machine-appliquéd to a heavy cotton fabric. On the opposite side it reads FOOD NOW. A large safety pin holds the top together and serves as a handle by which the lunch can be carried to the table or to a bench in the sun.

The dimensions of this bag are 7½″ (19.1 cm) wide, 11″ (27.9 cm) high, and 4″ (10.2 cm) deep, and it is made according to Basic Tote #1 (page 122), with the following variations:

1. Cut tote piece 8½″ by 28″ (21.6 cm by 71.1 cm). Cut 2 side panels 12½″ by 4″ (31.8 cm by 10.2 cm). Cut no handles.
2. Finish appliqué on flat fabrics.
3. After assembly, turn under ½″ (12 mm) of top edge and press. Then turn down another ½″ (12 mm) and topstitch or slip-stitch to bag.

Recycled Denim Tote

This decorative tote includes an entire collection of approaches to surface embellishment. Appliqué, embroidery, machine stitching, buttons, and beads all contribute texture and pattern.

Appliqué, embroidery, and buttons all add decorative details to this denim and bandanna print tote.

A special brown bag for workshops or all-day meetings. By Carole Austin.

Karen Bray made this tote rigid and added to its versatility by inserting a portion of a large plastic bottle. The top of the bottle was cut off and the fabric was measured around the plastic to determine the actual size needed. The plastic was slipped inside the bag after parts were joined and after the lining was sewn in. That way the plastic can be removed for cleaning.

The construction shown in Basic Tote #7 (page 134) was used for this carryall. The casing is sewn so that there is a space above it, making a gathered top. This tote can be made following the instructions given for the rainbow lunch bag on page 61.

Sit-on Tote

If you've worn sparkly white pants to the tennis meet, and the bleachers look a bit dusty, here's a tote to keep you clean. A brief rest on any grassy area or park bench may be more comfortable if you can relax and forget about dust and dirt.

This tote is 17″ (43.2 cm) wide by 13″ (33 cm) high. Follow these directions:

A simple carryall tote opens to provide a seat.

The inside pockets of this traveling companion hold games, paper tablets, and colored pencils to fill hours of travel time. By Gloria McNutt. (Photo by Jean Ray Laury)

boy's pet white rat can company him in this special rrier. By Carole Austin. hoto by Stan Bitters)

A cardboard carton covered with fabric is made into a special tote for gardeners. (Photo by Jean Ray Laury)

A festive bushel basket holds all the goodies for an outing. (Photo by Stan Bitters)

Scraps and remnants cover a cutoff gallon bleach bottle in this tote by Karen Bray. (Photo by Stan Bitters)

Fabric and naugahyde handles transform a box into a picnic tote. (Photo by Jean Ray Laury)

1. Cut all tote and lining pieces according to the pattern which includes a ½″ (12-mm) seam allowance. Sew lined pockets to tote back as shown. Finished patch is 8″ by 15″ (20.3 cm by 38.1 cm). Make according to directions on page 152.

2. Place 1 side piece and 1 side lining piece with wrong sides together. Pin and baste. Bind long edge with bias tape or other fabric binding. (If you use lining fabric for the binding, cut a strip 1½″ [3.8 cm] wide.) Repeat for other side piece, being sure that the tote fabric faces outside on each.

3. Place front and back tote material and lining material together with wrong sides facing. Baste at outside edge.

4. Cut 2 handles. Sew as directed in the section on handles beginning page 146.

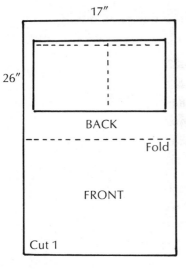

17″
26″
BACK
Fold
FRONT
Cut 1

5. Pin handles with raw ends matching top edge of tote as in the drawing. Handles are centered, 4½″ (11.4 cm) apart.

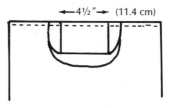

←—4½″—→ (11.4 cm)

6. Pin and baste raw edges of triangles to sides of tote. Sew close to outside edge.

7. Bind sides of tote, joining triangles to tote.

8. Bind top and bottom edges, catching handles in seam.

9. Tuck side panels to inside for an ample tote. Open, with pockets to the back, for sit-on.

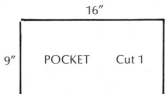

16″
9″   POCKET   Cut 1

Pattern for sit-on tote

4″ =	10.2 cm
9″ =	22.9 cm
12″ =	30.5 cm
15″ =	38.1 cm
16″ =	40.6 cm
17″ =	43.2 cm
26″ =	66 cm

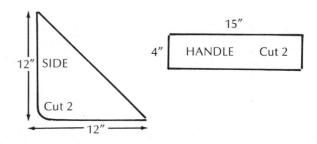

12″ SIDE
Cut 2
12″

15″
4″   HANDLE   Cut 2

7. Travel Totes

Packing, according to some expert travelers, is essentially a matter of organization. Here are ways to organize travel needs large and small. Tiny totes and roll-up totes keep jewelry, makeup, or vitamins in compact packets.

Clothes carriers, usually nondescript, can function just as well if they are elegant—and no stewardess will fail to remember your unique wardrobe carrier. Any totes or carriers of unusual design or unique decorative detail are very *unlikely* to be whisked away, either intentionally or unintentionally. A simple graphic design, a prominent monogram, or even a band of bright color will identify your gear unquestionably.

Travel Roll-up Tote

Here's a marvelous travel tote for necklaces, rings, scarves, hose, gloves, and other small articles. Each is separated and protected, providing quick access to them all. Follow the directions for Basic Tote #11 (page 142).

These pockets are 5" (12.7 cm) deep. The knitted panel here is backed with felt, but this tote can be made from any fabric. When not traveling, it stores any assortment of small items.

Travel Set

A brown duck garment bag is piped in purple and has a dazzling rainbow appliquéd in one corner. No one aboard the plane will confuse your garment bag with his or hers.

To make the bag, start with a wood hanger. Select one that you'll be using in the garment bag later. Trace the top edge of the hanger onto paper, extending the line 3" (7.6 cm) to 4" (10.2 cm) beyond the ends of the hanger. Drop a line straight down from that extension, making the bag as

Knitted pockets hold an array of small articles which are rolled up for packing. By Mark D. Law.

Traveler's garment bag has rainbow on back and zips up front for easy access to clothes. 24″ (61 cm) wide and 34″ (86.4 cm) long. The matching tote bag is huge and roomy and is designed to fit under the seat on an airliner.

long as needed depending upon whether you'll be carrying dresses, sport coats, or whatever. Use the pattern to cut 2 bag shapes. In one, sew a long zipper down the center—a 24″ (61-cm) one was used in this bag. Add a decorative design to the other side.

Stitch all outside edges together, then trim seam. Bind with contrasting color. Be sure to leave a small opening at the top through which to insert the hook of the hanger.

The shoulder bag matches the garment bag and has a matching rainbow on the reverse side. Inside and outside pockets hold tickets, luggage checks, and keys.

Finished size of tote is 20″ (50.8 cm) wide, 12″ (30.5 cm) high, and 3″ (7.6 cm) deep. To make, follow the directions given for Basic Tote #1 (page 122), with the following variations:

1. Cut front and back of tote and lining 20″ by 33″ (50.8 cm by 83.8 cm). Cut side panels 3″ by 12½″ (7.6 cm by 31.8 cm). A ½″ (12-mm) seam allowance is included. Cut handle strap 5″ by 50″ (12.7 cm by 127 cm).

2. Finish any appliqué, pockets, or graphics on flat tote pieces, before assembly.

3. Mark a fold line 6″ (15.2 cm) from one end for a flap. Round off corners of flap, using a large plate.

4. Place lining and tote material together. Baste at outside edge with wrong sides facing.

5. Set in side panels according to basic instructions. Allow 6″ (15.2 cm) of flap to extend at back.

6. Trim all seams. Bind raw edges with a fabric binding of contrasting color.

7. Sew handle straps and turn. Finish ends and make 3 lines of top stitching the length of strap.

8. Overlap straps on outside of tote sides.

All-Day Bag and Shaving Kit

Rope handles strung through grommets add dash to heavy cotton fabric. The zippered shaving kit travels with the all-day bag and carries a man's

Traveling duet of all-day bag and shaving kit is made so that one bag can slip inside the other, or they can be carried individually.

shaving gear or a woman's cosmetics. Grommets and rope are available in notions and yardage departments. The finished size of the bag is 12″ by 12″ by 5″ (30.5 cm by 30.5 cm by 12.7 cm). You will need four grommets and two 22″ (55.9-cm) rope handles. Rope is ⅜″ (9.5 mm) thick.

To make the all-day bag, follow directions for Basic Tote #1 (page 122), with these variations:

1. Cut tote panel 13½″ by 33″ (34.3 cm by 83.8 cm). Cut side insets 6″ by 14½″ (15.2 cm by 36.8 cm). Cut pocket 6½″ by 7½″ (16.5 cm by 19.1 cm).
2. Make according to basic pattern, sewing pocket on front of tote while fabric is flat.
3. After top edge of tote has been turned and topstitched, put grommets in hemmed area, spaced 4″ (10.2 cm) apart and centered.
4. Topstitch side edges where tote panel and side inset are seamed. Slip rope through grommets to inside and tie or knot each end to hold in place.

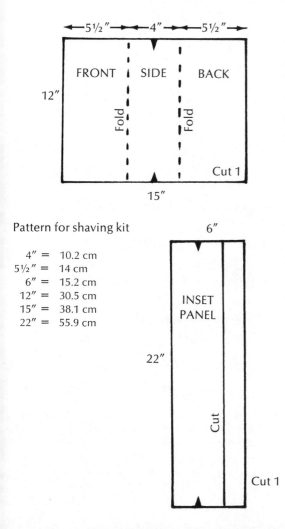

Pattern for shaving kit

4″ =	10.2 cm	
5½″ =	14 cm	
6″ =	15.2 cm	
12″ =	30.5 cm	
15″ =	38.1 cm	
22″ =	55.9 cm	

The shaving kit is really a cloth box with a zipper. The back and front and one side are formed by the larger panel. The inset panel with the zipper serves as the other side, top, and bottom. You will need a 12″ (30.5-cm) zipper, two grommets, and 18″ (45.7 cm) of rope.

1. Cut front, side, and back panel 12″ by 15″ (30.5 cm by 38.1 cm). Cut inset panel 6″ by 22″ (15.2 cm by 55.9 cm). This pattern includes a ½″ (12-mm) seam allowance.
2. Cut inset panel lengthwise 2″ (5.1 cm) from one edge. Seam the cut edges 9″ (22.9 cm) from one end.

Inset zipper in rest of opening. Side inset should measure 5″ by 22″ (12.7 cm by 55.9 cm) after zipper has been added.

3. Sew inset panel to tote, right sides together, matching the notches at end of inset to center of 15″ (38.1-cm) side of tote. Clip at corners as needed. Leave zipper partially open for turning.

4. Turn. Topstitch at edge where tote panel and side inset are seamed.

5. Set grommets into tote panel at top center, 1″ (2.5 cm) from top edge. Slip ends of rope through grommets and knot on inside.

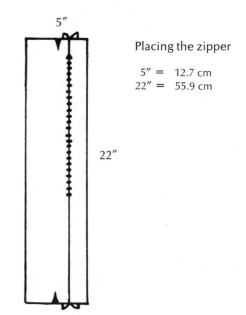

Placing the zipper

5″ = 12.7 cm
22″ = 55.9 cm

Pill Tote

For traveling, here is a roll-up tote to carry vitamins, medications, or aspirin. The designer, Joan Lewis, has made six compartments in Basic Tote #11 (page 142), claiming that anyone needing more is probably in too precarious a state of health to travel!

In this tote, 2 pieces of fabric 18″ by 23″ (45.7 cm by 58.4 cm) provide a backing piece. They are sewn, right sides together, on all 4 sides but with an opening to turn the material right side out. The opening is slip-stitched shut. Pockets are made by first piecing together a backing panel of solid-colored fabrics the width needed for finished pockets. They will vary according to specific needs, but the finished sizes of these vary from 3″ (7.6 cm) wide to 4″ (10.2 cm) wide. When these are pieced together, they make a rectangle 5″ by 15″ (12.7 cm by 38.1 cm). The strip is joined to the large backing with padding between the 2 layers. Pockets are cut larger, then joined in the same way. Top stitching secures pockets to backing panel.

With top and bottom folded over, the pill tote is rolled up to prevent any bottles from slipping out of place.

Vitamins and medicines are
slipped into pockets for safe travel
in this pill tote.

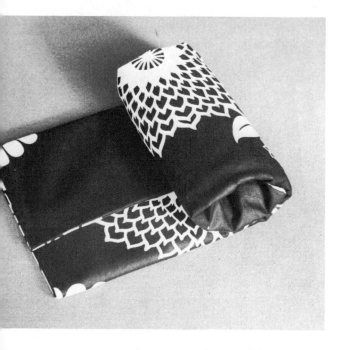

This tote is attached to a belt, freeing the cyclist's hands and keeping essentials within reach.

Cyclist's Tote

Both motorcyclists and bicycle riders need a tote that leaves hands free for driving. This simple envelope tote takes less than an hour to make, and if it is made of vinyl, serves double duty as a rain tote.

The finished size is 8″ (20.3 cm) wide by 7½″ (19.1 cm) high, including channel for belt. Follow instructions given in Basic Tote #3 (page 126), with the following variations:

1. Cut tote and lining according to the pattern.
2. Sew lining to tote as instructed.

```
          9″
     ┌──────────┐  ↑
     │          │
18″  │  FLAP    │ 5½″
     │          │  ↓
     ├ ─ ─ ─ ─ ─┤  ↑
Fold │          │
     │          │
     │  BACK    │ 7½″
     │          │
     │          │  ↓
     ├ ─ ─ ─ ─ ─┤  ↑
Fold │          │
     │  FRONT   │ 5″
     │          │  ↓
     └──────────┘
  Cut 1
```

Pattern for cyclist's tote

5″	=	12.7 cm
5½″	=	14 cm
7½″	=	19.1 cm
9″	=	22.9 cm
18″	=	45.7 cm

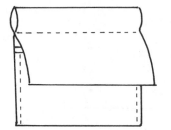

3. Fold bottom edge up on fold line and topstitch sides only.
4. Fold top down on fold line and topstitch 1½″ (3.8 cm) below fold to make channel for belt as in the drawing.

Runaway Totes

The simple drawstring totes simplify weekend-excursion packing. Plan a different-colored tote for each youngster and he or she will find it easier to keep track of sneakers, favorite teddy bears, and books. Drawstrings automatically close bags when they're lifted and provide over-the-shoulder hoisting. Use iron-on tape for decorative designs.

Follow directions for Basic Tote #6 (page 131), varying sizes according to need. Middle-sized bag on left is tied according to Variation A (page 132). The large one at center is made like the his and hers totes (page 91).

Drawstring totes are perfect for "quick getaway" packing.
From 8″ by 12″ (20.3 cm by 30.1 cm) to 18″ by 24″ (45.7 cm by 61 cm).

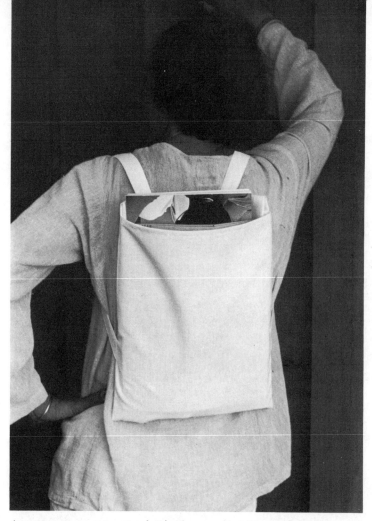

An easy way to get around, whether you're hiking, biking, or taking the youngsters on an outing. By Janice Rosenberg.

Backpack

An envelope-type tote is changed into a backpack with the addition of straps.

Finished size is 11″ wide by 14″(27.9 cm by 35.6 cm). Follow instructions for Basic Tote #3 (page 126), with the following variations:

1. Cut tote (lining optional) 12″ by 35″ (30.5 cm by 88.9 cm), following the pattern.
2. Turn under ½″ (12 mm) and topstitch the two 12″ (30.5-cm) ends, turning edges to inside.

Backpack pattern showing the placement of the straps

6½″ =	16.5 cm
12″ =	30.5 cm
14″ =	35.6 cm
14½″ =	36.8 cm
35″ =	88.9 cm

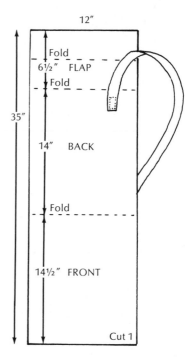

3. Cut 2 straps 23″ by 3″ (58.4 cm by 7.6 cm). Sew according to directions for turned handles on page 146. Finish ends on each.
4. Insert strap ends in side seams according to the pattern. Pin.
5. Sew finished ends to top of tote, just past the fold for flap, as shown in the pattern.
6. Turn down top fold line to 3½″ (8.9 cm) and topstitch.
7. With right sides together, join side seams. Turn.

Jewelry Tote

Very small items have a way of sliding out of suitcase pockets. Here's a knitted bag that solves the dilemma of what to do with "little tinies." The drawstring is pulled tight and tied, and the bright-colored tote is easily located among your clothes.

Make similar totes from leather, suede cloth, or knits, following the instructions for Basic Tote #6 (page 131). The tiny totes are delightful in bright prints, quilted fabrics, or felts.

Tiny knitted tote with ribbon drawstring and ball fringe tucks jewelry safely amid suitcase packing. By Mark D. Law.

8. Rainproof Totes

A rainy day brings forth special rain gear—slickers, umbrellas, and, naturally, rain totes. Plastics and vinyls, available in bright, shiny colors, add to the range of choices as do waterproofed materials of all kinds. Flaps help protect the contents, and various small inside or outside pockets prevent soaking delays while you search for keys or change.

Striped Rain Tote

Stripes, cut on the diagonal, are used in this over-the-shoulder rain tote. Handles go around the bag for extra support and are short enough so that it can be carried by hand.

The finished size of this tote is 11″ (27.9 cm) wide, 12″ (30.5 cm) high, and 3″ (7.6 cm) deep. Handles extend 20″ (50.8 cm) above the top of the bag. Make it according to the Basic Tote #2 (page 124), with the following variations:

1. Cut tote and lining according to the pattern.
2. Cut handle strap 2½″ by 92″ (6.4 cm by 233.7 cm). (Piece as necessary. If just 2 lengths are needed, it can be pieced so that seams go at the

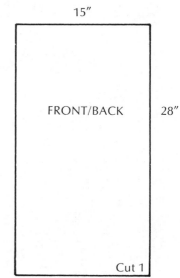

Pattern for
striped rain tote

7″ = 17.8 cm
12″ = 30.5 cm
15″ = 38.1 cm
28″ = 71.1 cm

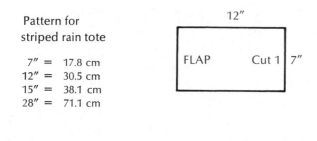

Bright, candy-striped vinyl adds color to even the gloomiest rainy day.

bottom of the bag.) See page 146 for directions on topstitched handles. Baste or glue handles with fabric glue. Do not topstitch them at this time.

3. Position handle on the flat tote as in the drawing. Center handle lengthwise so strap loops extend equally over ends of tote. Machine-stitch to tote with a reinforced stitch at each end, as shown on page 148. Then topstitch loose sections of handles.

4. With right sides together stitch side seams of tote panel.

5. Box bottom as in basic pattern with a 3″ (7.6-cm) box (sewn line is 1½″ [3.8 cm] from corner).

6. With right sides facing, center 12″ (30.5-cm) edge of flap piece to top edge of tote back and sew together. Press open.

7. Turn edges of flap and tote top to inside ½″ (12 mm) and press. Clip at corners. Repeat for lining and press.

8. Slip lining into tote. Pin or baste all folded edges together and topstitch.

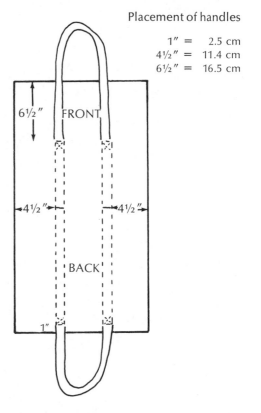

Placement of handles

1″ =	2.5 cm
4½″ =	11.4 cm
6½″ =	16.5 cm

FRONT

6½″

4½″   4½″

BACK

1″

Rain Tote

By means of a large flap, this spacious tote offers ample protection for the contents in a downpour. The plastic vinyl exterior and the handle strap are lined in a brightly striped cotton.

A variation of the envelope type of construction makes this tote a simple one to assemble. The finished bag shown is 13″ (33 cm) wide by 18″ (45.7 cm) high. The strap extends 30″ (76.2 cm) above top of bag. Use these, or select your own measurements, and follow instructions for Basic Tote #3 (page 126), with the following variations:

1. Cut tote and lining according to the pattern.
2. Sew lining to tote with right sides together, leaving an opening at the straight end for turning. Turn, fold under the seam allowance at the open end, then topstitch.
3. Make handle and attach to the tote fabric as indicated by dotted lines in the pattern. Sew through handle, tote, and lining. Then fold bag at fold line A and topstitch sides. Fold at line B to make a flap.

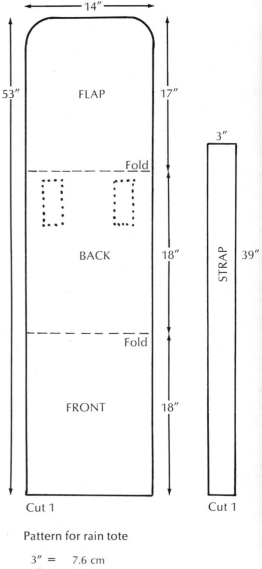

Pattern for rain tote

3″	=	7.6 cm
14″	=	35.6 cm
17″	=	43.2 cm
18″	=	45.7 cm
39″	=	99.1 cm
53″	=	134.6 cm

Bike Backpack

Bikers have slightly different tote needs, since both hands must be kept free for the handlebars. Here's a pack that serves as well in the sun as in the rain. A band across the tote front holds the flap closed and serves as a panel for initials. To add the letters see page 155.

Shiny yellow vinyl rain tote has a huge flap to keep out drenching rain.

Waterproof canvas lets biker carry books for class even through the rain.

The finished size of this pack is 10½″ (26.7 cm) wide, 12″ (30.5 cm) high, and 4″ (10.2 cm) deep. It has two straps, each 22″ (55.9 cm) from top of bag to side. Make this pack according to Basic Tote #1 (page 122), with the following variations:

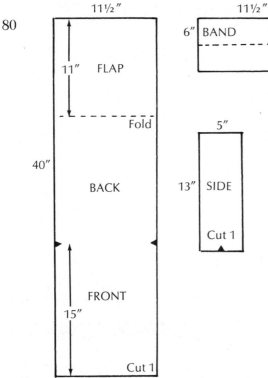

11½"

6" | BAND | Cut 1
Fold

11" FLAP

Fold

40"

5"

BACK

13" | SIDE

Cut 1

FRONT

15"

Cut 1

Pattern for bike backpack

5"	=	12.7 cm	13"	=	33 cm
6"	=	15.2 cm	15"	=	38.1 cm
11"	=	27.9 cm	40"	=	101.6 cm
11½"	=	29.2 cm			

1. Cut according to pattern which includes ½" (12-mm) seam allowance.
2. Use two 1½" by 40" (3.8-cm by 101.6-cm) woven straps (available at tent and awning suppliers, mountaineering shops, or army surplus). The drawing shows placement of straps.
3. Topstitch straps to back of tote while fabric is flat, leaving them loose for length adjustment.
4. Assemble according to basic directions, except leave top 1" (2.5 cm) of seam open when joining side panels to back of tote.
5. Turn top edges of tote front and sides under ½" (12 mm) and machine-stitch. Turn another ½" (12 mm) and topstitch.
6. Turn flap edges under ¼" (6 mm) and stitch. Turn another ¼" (6 mm) and topstitch.
7. Adjust strap lengths and stitch each to the top of the tote back, overlapping ends onto previously sewn straps. Topstitch and reinforce.
8. Fold band in half lengthwise, right sides facing, and sew 1 end and side together. Turn through open end and press. Turn raw edges of open end to inside ½" (12 mm) and blindstitch closed.
9. Adjust placement to tote front so band holds the flap easily. Topstitch to edge of tote.

Placement of straps

| 2" | = | 5.1 cm |
| 11" | = | 27.9 cm |

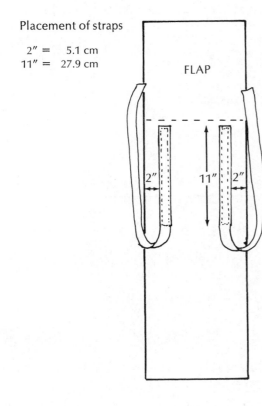

FLAP

2" 11" 2"

Shoe Bag

Even puddle-jumping doesn't always keep your feet dry when there's a downpour. Here's a tote sized (10″ by 13″ [25.4 cm by 33 cm]) to just fit an extra pair of shoes. Lined in bright yellow print (a washable cotton) this red vinyl bag sheds water with ease. Make it according to Basic Tote #5 (page 130), or use the following variations:

1. Cut tote and lining pieces 11″ by 15″ (27.9 cm by 38.1 cm).
2. Cut 2 handle straps 4″ by 15″ (10.2 cm by 38.1 cm).
3. Sew side and bottom seams of tote material.
4. Sew only side seams of lining.
5. Make handles according to the instructions on page 146. Center handles, one on each side of tote top. Pin handles to vinyl, raw ends matching, and stitch ¼″ (6 mm) from edge.
6. Place lining and tote material with right sides facing and pin around the top edge of tote. Baste, then machine-stitch.
7. Turn, push lining into bag so that top 1″ (2.5 cm) of tote folds over to inside.
8. Measure distance to bottom of tote. Pull lining out and topstitch the bottom seam.

Vinyl-coated fabric is ideal for the extra pair of shoes invariably needed during the rainy season.

9. Sewing Totes

Sewing of every kind is going more places than ever before, so special totes are in demand.

Needlepointers stitch away in committee meetings or while waiting for the cat at the vet's. Crewel embroiderers sew while listening to the news on TV or in the waiting room at the dentist's office. These patches of time make the difference between finished and unfinished projects in any busy schedule. Even mending is more likely to be accomplished if everything is together whenever a few spare moments present themselves.

Stitchers find that an assortment of small things, including needle case, spools of thread, scissors, flosses, beeswax, and thimbles, need to be kept in one place. Then when the stitcher takes off for a meeting, an afternoon visit, a workshop, or a class, all the tools are ready.

Some sewing totes allow ample space to include the stitchery project or needlepoint in progress. Others are a means of organizing the tools only. Most of these are designed by women who sew and therefore the totes meet their specific needs beautifully.

Sewing Pocket

Two fabric pieces form the front and back of this very practical and decorative sewing pocket. You can make your own, following the general instructions for Basic Tote #5 (page 130), or make this one as follows:

1. Cut tote and lining pieces according to the pattern which includes a ½″ (12-mm) seam allowance. If the lining is to be patchwork, like this one, do the piecing first. Then cut pattern pieces from it.
2. Baste linings to tote pieces, right sides facing out.
3. Cut a 6″ (15.2-cm) opening in front of tote as shown. Cut through tote and lining. Bind raw edges with bias strip or bias tape.

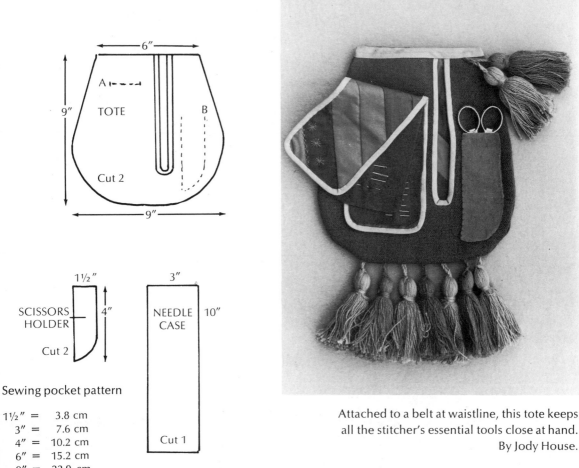

1½"

SCISSORS
HOLDER   4"

Cut 2

3"

NEEDLE
CASE   10"

Cut 1

Sewing pocket pattern

1½" = 3.8 cm
3" = 7.6 cm
4" = 10.2 cm
6" = 15.2 cm
9" = 22.9 cm
10" = 25.4 cm

Attached to a belt at waistline, this tote keeps
all the stitcher's essential tools close at hand.
By Jody House.

4. Finish needle case by basting tote and lining material together. Bind all edges. Place a 2½" by 4" (6.4 cm by 10.2 cm) strip of felt across the middle of needle case. Lay on top of the tote front, topstitch through center to attach needle case to bag at A.

5. The scissors holder is made from 2 pieces of material stitched with right sides together at sides and bottom. Turn. Slip-stitch top edge. Slip-stitch to tote at B.

6. Front and back are joined with lining and facing, then turned. If fringes are added, insert them in the outside seam as front and back are stitched together. Finally, bind the top edge. A wide grosgrain ribbon sewn to the back provides a channel to slip the sewing pocket over a belt. Or ties may be added so that the pocket can be secured, apron-like, around the waist.

Sewing Tote

This handy carryall sewing bag has wood dowel handles for easy toting. Dowels also stiffen the edge so bag doesn't slump or crumple. The stiff upholstery fabric used here gives the bag body enough to stand upright.

The finished size of this tote is 15″ (38.1 cm) wide, 14″ (35.6 cm) high, and 6″ (15.2 cm) deep. It is made like Basic Tote #1 (page 122), with the following variations:

1. Cut tote panel 16″ by 37″ (40.6 cm by 94 cm), sides 7″ by 14″ (17.8 cm by 35.6 cm). Sew according to basic tote.
2. Side panel will be 1½″ (3.8 cm) shorter than front panel.
3. Cut a rectangle out of center top each side, 5″ (12.7 cm) down and 4″ (10.2 cm) across.
4. Bind rectangle edges with binding or bias tape. Topstitch.
5. Turn down top edge to make channels for wood dowels. Hem and topstitch.
6. Slip in dowels and sew channel ends closed.

Sewing tote is easy to carry and opens wide to reveal its deepest recesses.

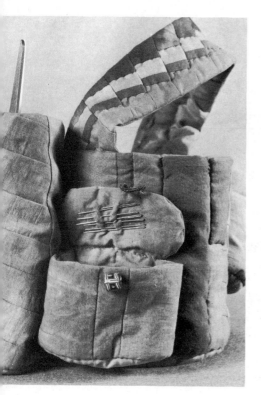

Piecing and Seminole patchwork are combined in this tote of fabric cylinders. By Vicki Johnson.

Padded Sewing Tote

Anyone who ever carries mending or sewing needs a tote like this. Easy access to all compartments makes it a cinch to pick up scissors or fabrics in a moment. Smaller pockets, some lidded, provide containers for thimbles, pincushions, needles, and threads.

Seminole patchwork was used to add decorative details. Other fabrics are hand-dyed. All decorative piecing and padding are completed on the fabric while it is flat. Then the fabric parts are joined to form the tote.

Assorted sizes of Basic Tote #7 (page 134) were made and blindstitched together to make this tote. The largest cylinder is 5″ (12.7 cm) wide by 6″ (15.2 cm) high.

Patchwork shows that this tote belongs to a teacher of needlework.
Sides are not stitched so that the tote can be opened flat.

Embroiderer's Tote

This sewing bag, opened up flat, reveals all the supplies used by the needlepointer or crewel stitcher. The pockets can easily be varied to fit other specific needs.

Gail Giberson designed this tote to take sewing materials to her classes or traveling. By completing the patchwork first, the tote shape can be determined. The octagonal shape used here resulted from her patchwork design. Using the patchwork block as a pattern, the tote shape was cut, slightly larger, in the polka-dot fabric. The material was folded at the bottom. The lining was cut to same size.

The pockets and containers were sewn to the lining. Patchwork was appliquéd to the front tote piece. An additional piece of polka-dot fabric was then cut and sewn to fit the handles. It was folded over the handles and stitched. Fabric portions of handles were inserted between top seam of the tote and lining when they were joined.

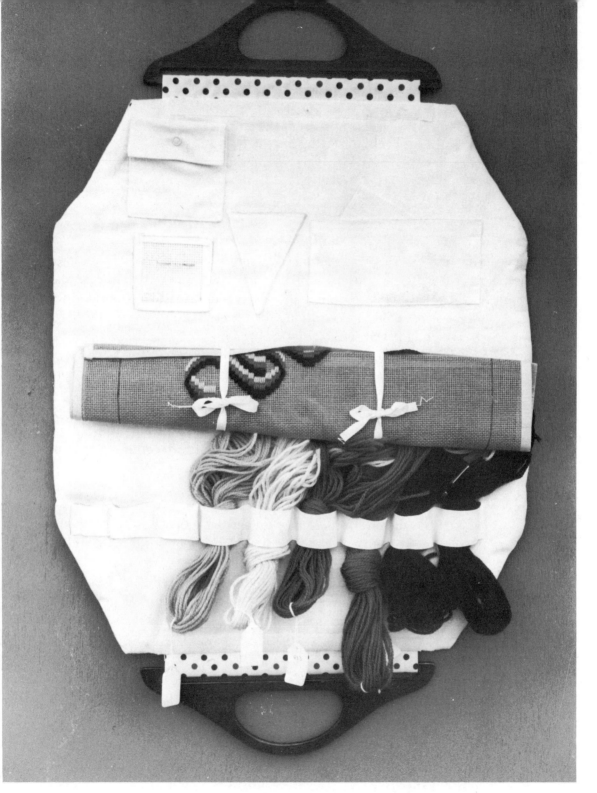

Opened, this tote lies flat and the needleworker finds all tools within easy reach.

10. Sport Totes

Few activities require as much toting as do sports of all kinds. Here are totes designed especially for various sports—tennis, swimming, gymnastics, and more. Adapt these totes to your particular needs by making pockets for certain objects, or adding plastic lining for waterproofing.

Some are designed with the thought of keeping both hands free—as with totes or backpacks for cyclists. Others are amply large to carry a complete change of clothes so that tennis shoes and shorts or swimsuit and towel are packed and ready to go when you are. Even more passive activities, like bird-watching and photography, need special carriers—the wild-flower buff needs a way to carry books for identification and a magnifying glass. The budding entomologist wants a means of carrying and protecting specimens.

Quilted Tennis Tote

This over-the-shoulder tennis bag carries everything essential to the court. A very versatile bag, it is not limited to the tennis buff. It could as easily hold leotards and dance slippers, or schoolbooks and papers.

It is 14" (35.6 cm) square, finished, and handles extend 34" (86.4 cm) above the top of bag. It is made according to Basic Tote #2 (page 124), with the following variations:

1. Cut tote piece 19" by 36" (48.3 cm by 91.4 cm). Repeat for lining if used.
2. Sew giant pocket, finished at 13" (33 cm) wide and 12" (30.5 cm) high, to front of bag, before stitching side seams. Top edge should be 3" (7.6 cm) from cut end of bag, parallel to the 19" (48.3-cm) edge. This tote has fabric-shop embroidered stars added along with prefinished white piping at edge of pocket. A 38" (96.5-cm) length of piping is required.
3. Follow basic directions for assembly. Box to make sides 4" (10.2 cm) deep, leaving front of bag 14" (35.6 cm) wide.

A quilted blue denim bag holds a change of clothes while tennis racket fits into pocket on the outside.

4. Cut 2 handles, 38″ by 4″ (96.5 cm by 10.2 cm). Sew according to directions for handles beginning on page 146. Attach at inside.

Tennis Tote

Pockets inside and out provide spaces for everything. The racket is zipped into a racket-head-shaped pocket, and small pockets in the interior hold billfold, car keys, or change.

The finished size of the tote is 20″ (50.8 cm) wide, 15″ (38.1 cm) high, and 6″ (15.2 cm) deep. The construction follows that of Basic Tote #1 (page 122), with the following variations:

1. Cut 1 tote panel 20″ by 36″ (50.8 cm by 91.4 cm). Cut 2 side panels 6″ by 14″ (15.2 cm by 35.6 cm).

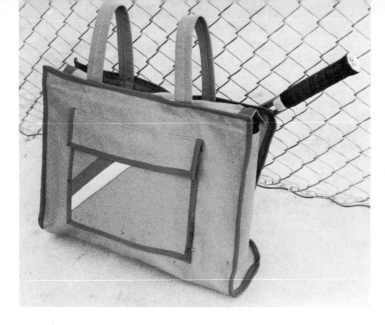

Bright blue canvas with bound seams and outside pocket makes up this carryall for the court. By Bea Slater.

2. While tote material is flat, add pockets and racket holder. The pocket is 9″ (22.9 cm) high by 12″ (30.5 cm) wide, with a 3″ by 12″ (7.6 cm by 30.5 cm) flap covering the opening.

3. To make racket holder, trace around racket, then add 1″ (2.5 cm) all the way around. Attach with woven binding, using a 9″ (22.9-cm) zipper to join racket holder to tote at top.

4. Sew all seams with wrong sides of fabric together. Trim seams and bind with a ready-made woven binding from fabric shop.

5. Cut 2 panels 3″ by 20″ (7.6 cm by 50.8 cm) with the 20″ (50.8-cm) lengths on the selvage. Set an 18″ (45.7-cm) zipper between them length-

The taped and zippered pocket for the racket head.

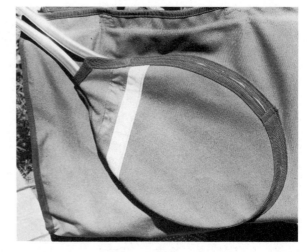

wise, using selvage edges on sides of zipper (do not turn under a seam allowance by zipper). Join panel together at both ends of zipper with woven binding.

6. Open zipper. With right sides together, join zippered panel to top edges of tote, just 1″ (2.5 cm) under top binding.
7. Add straps, finished size 1½″ by 16″ (3.8 cm by 40.6 cm), machine-stitching to the wrong side of tote between zipper panel and top edge. The handles are spaced 5″ (12.7 cm) in from outside edges.

His and Hers Totes

Drawstring totes, in dazzling colors, are identified with lettering. These letters are made with iron-on tape which is a quick and easy method.

The bags are made in a finished size of 17″ (43.2 cm) wide by 24″

Immense drawstring bags help you haul it all in one trip.

(61 cm) high, according to directions for Basic Tote #6 (page 131), with the following variations:

1. Cut tote panel 35″ by 29″ (88.9 cm by 73.7 cm).
2. Join the 35″ (88.9-cm) edges, leaving the top 4½″ (11.4 cm) open. Join bottom edges. Press seams open. Turn under ¼″ (6 mm) at each raw edge of the 4½″ (11.4-cm) opening. Finish by topstitching.
3. Apply decorative lettering.

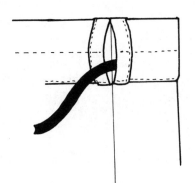

4. Fold top edge of tote to outside, folding under ½″ (12 mm) and stitching. Fold top edge down another 4″ (10.2 cm). Baste. Stitch ¼″ (6 mm) from hem edge. Then add another row of stitching 2″ (5.1 cm) above that. Run cord through for drawstring as in the drawing. Use a 60″ (152.4-cm) drawstring cord which doubles as a shoulder strap.

Swim and Gym Tote

Here's a tote that youngsters love to use and carry. It is made over a cylindrical cardboard box from the ice-cream store. Use any similar cylindrical container or plastic bucket.

The tote pictured here is 9½″ (24.1 cm) across (cut base circle 10½″ [26.7 cm]). A 32″ (81.3-cm) length of fabric is needed to wrap around. Cut your pattern from a box as indicated in the directions for Basic Tote #7 (page 134), with the following variations:

1. Cut according to individual needs.
2. Join as directed, piecing colors if you prefer.
3. Finish top edge by turning under ¼″ (6 mm) and stitching. Or use selvage as in the tote in the photograph.
4. Sew a strip of fabric (cut 2½″ by 33″ [6.4 cm by 83.9 cm] for this tote) and turn under ½″ (12 mm) at each long edge. Baste. Turn under 1″ (2.5 cm) at ends and topstitch.
5. Baste and stitch this band of fabric on the outside top edge of tote, 2″

A three-gallon ice-cream carton provides the base for this carryall.

The resident of a tree house, above, carries lunch up the tree in this tote.

(5.1 cm) from top edge. Leave ends open. This forms a channel for a drawstring.

6. Corded cotton, 36″ (91.4 cm) long, provides drawstring and handle here.

Sport Tote

A square box makes this bag hold its shape and protects the contents. And the jungle-print fabric gives it great appeal for small fry. It will carry all the gear for gym or swimming.

The carryall is made following directions for Basic Tote #12 (page 143), Variation (page 145). The box is 10″ (25.4 cm) square and the tote is 17″ (43.2 cm) high.

Huge beach bags swallow bulky, large beach towels and beach gear.

To the Beach

A gigantic drawstring tote, nearly 36″ (91.4 cm) tall, absorbs all the beach gear for the trip back to cabin or car. The smaller bag keeps lotions, oils, and tanning aids separated.

Each bag is decorated in fabric applied with iron-on bonding material. These totes are made according to the directions for his and hers totes (page 91). Alter the sizes to suit personal preferences, but the procedures are identical. The larger bag is 34″ by 24″ (86.4 cm by 61 cm). The smaller one is 19″ by 12″ (48.3 cm by 30.5 cm).

Biker's Bag

Slip this side-hugging tote over head and shoulder, then a sweater or jacket can be worn over the top. Bicyclists will enjoy this bag since it leaves

This small bag fits over the shoulder. Great for bikers.

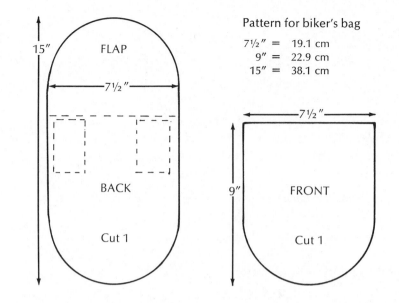

Pattern for biker's bag

7½" = 19.1 cm
9" = 22.9 cm
15" = 38.1 cm

FLAP

15"

7½"

BACK

Cut 1

7½"

9"

FRONT

Cut 1

both hands free. Anyone would find this type of carrier handy—children can't lose the bag and it's great to have at a carnival or an amusement park for those times when you need to hang on with both hands.

The finished size of this bag is 6½" (15.2 cm) wide by 9" (22.9 cm) high, with handles extending 35" (88.9 cm) from top of bag. Follow directions for Basic Tote #5 (page 130). Variations from basic directions are as follows:

1. Cut bag and lining as shown in pattern. Cut a handle and handle lining 3" by 45" (7.6 cm by 114.3 cm).
2. Place tote and lining pieces for back/flap sections with right sides together. Pin or baste, sew edges, leaving a 3" (7.6-cm) opening. Trim seam and turn to right side. Turn under raw edges of opening and baste shut.
3. Sew tote and lining pieces for flap with right sides facing, leaving the straight top edge open. Turn.
4. Bind raw edges of straight end with bias tape or lining fabric.
5. Sew handle and handle lining together, right sides facing. Turn. Finish ends. Stitch to back of tote with finished end 5" (12.7 cm) below fold line as indicated on the pattern. Stitch to fold line.
6. Place tote front piece over tote back, linings facing. Baste, then topstitch sides and bottom. Turn down flap on the fold line which is ½" (12 mm) above the top edge of tote front.

Colorfully marked garment bag
and travel tote won't get lost.
(Photo by Jean Ray Laury)

Rope handles and grommeted
canvas make a sturdy traveling set.
(Photo by Jean Ray Laury)

Pockets hold pill bottles of all shapes in a roll-up travel tote.
By Joan Lewis. (Photo by Stan Bitters)

Drawstring totes with iron-on tape appliqués simplify an unscheduled trip. (Photo by Jean Ray Laury)

Hand-dyed fabric and patchwork cylinders make this sewing basket by Vicki Johnson. (Photo by Gayle Smalley)

All the gear for a tennis game fits in this zippered canvas tote by Bea Slater. (Photo by Jean Ray Laury)

Here's a nature lover's tote carried easily over the arm. All necessities for identifying rare species are at hand.

Bird-Watcher's Bag

A simple, straightforward tote balances well over a wide handle. It has a surprising capacity, since it is boxed.

To adapt this tote to your own special needs, add pockets inside and out, or use decorative appliqué and embroidery to define the nature of its special use. Here, contrasting colors exaggerate the structure of the bag.

Make this tote exactly according to directions for Basic Tote #4 (page 128). The finished size is 13″ (33 cm) high, 12½″ (31.8 cm) wide, and 3½″ (8.9 cm) deep.

Camera Tote

Soft synthetic leather is used for this camera carrier. The straps serve to close the top as well as to provide a shoulder strap.

Duffel-type camera carrier
has grommeted top
for drawstring strap.

This duffel is made according to directions for the one-piece boxed tote. The finished size is 6″ (15.2 cm) wide, 11″ (27.9 cm) high, and 6″ (15.2 cm) deep. Follow procedure for Basic Tote #2 (page 124), with the following variations:

1. Cut strap 2″ by 75″ (5.1 cm by 190.5 cm). Cut tote 13″ by 32″ (33 cm by 81.3 cm). Join side seams. Box corners to form 6″ (15.2-cm) bottom by stitching 3″ (7.6 cm) from corner point as in basic pattern.
2. Turn top edge to inside, folding down 2″ (5.1 cm). Pin and topstitch.
3. Put 8 grommets in bag (see page 155), spacing them so that folds are held in place when cording is run through.
4. Make strap by folding synthetic leather edges to meet at center and top-stitching.

5. Slip through grommets and determine the length of the strap section that runs through grommet area. Remove and fold in half lengthwise that section of strap and stitch together to form a more cordlike strap to slip easily through grommets.
6. Put strap back through grommets and stitch ends together.

Winged Feet

No jogger wants a bag to interfere with his or her trek around the neighborhood, and almost all sweat suits and warm-up suits are pocketless. So here's a solution for the fleet-footed. Robbie Fanning has devised a felt ankle tote which Mercury might have sported. The strap wraps around the ankle and closes with Velcro dots. The winged portion is a pocket to contain the house key, a dime for a phone call, or (in case of exhaustion) a bus ticket. The top of that portion also closes with Velcro dots.

Jogger's tote holds the house key.

II. Duffels and Sleeping Bag Carriers

As entertaining and houseguesting become more and more casual, there is a greater need for duffels and sleeping bag carriers. Whether the bag is to be tossed into the trunk of the car or checked through with luggage on your air flight, protection from dust and dirt is the greatest concern. Identification is undoubtedly a close second.

Sleeping bags are an almost essential part of a traveler's luggage, especially among easy-travel young people today. There is little doubt that the bag provides a moneysaving and timesaving element. So, whether traveling by plane, car, bus, or thumb, the sleeping bag needs to be toted and protected.

Two types of totes are given here, one a duffel type and the other a boxed variety. Remember that the drawstring tote shown in Basic Tote #6 (page 131) also makes a superb and easily sewn sleeping bag tote.

Another way of making a sleeping bag duffel is to follow the directions for a cylinder-type tote, as in Basic Tote #7 (page 134). Set a circle in as the base, then use a drawstring closure at the other end. The need for a zipper is eliminated.

Red Duffel

The duffel bag in brilliant shiny vinyl can be checked through with any luggage. Other fabrics can be substituted for vinyl, which is not easy to sew. The vinyl surface tends to stick to the sewing machine. Placing a piece of smooth or slick paper on the flat working area of the sewing machine will help ease the job. A double-feeding machine also assists in getting the two layers of vinyl fed through the machine at the same speed.

To make this tote, follow these directions:

1. Cut tote pieces according to the pattern which includes a ½″ (12-mm) seam allowance. Lining is not required. Vinyl, canvas, duck, or similar

Shiny red vinyl makes it easy to spot your own sleeping bag tote among the hundreds of suitcases arriving on any airliner. 22″ by 12″ (55.9 cm by 30.5 cm).

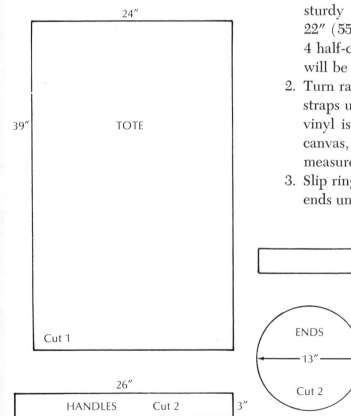

sturdy material is recommended. A 22″ (55.9-cm) heavy-duty zipper and 4 half-circle rings 1¾″ (4.5 cm) wide will be needed.

2. Turn raw edges of the 36″ (91.5-cm) straps under to meet in the center. If vinyl is used, glue edges down. For canvas, press and baste. Straps will measure 1½″ (3.8 cm) wide.

3. Slip rings on ends of each strap. Fold ends under 1½″ (3.8 cm) and baste or

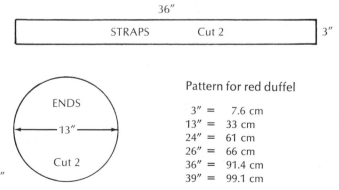

Pattern for red duffel

3″ =	7.6 cm
13″ =	33 cm
24″ =	61 cm
26″ =	66 cm
36″ =	91.4 cm
39″ =	99.1 cm

topstitch 1 line across strap to hold ring in place until sewing to tote.

4. Position straps on tote as in the drawing and topstitch in place with a reinforce stitch at each end next to rings as described on page 148.

5. Sew zipper to one of the 24″ (61-cm) ends of tote. Bring other 24″ (61-cm) end to zipper and sew so that zipper joins the 2 ends forming a cylinder. A small tab about 2″ by 2″ (5.1 cm by 5.1 cm) square, finished, can be topstitched on tote at end of zipper to close seam.

6. With right sides together, pin circular ends of tote to bag sides and stitch. Leave zipper partially open for turning. Turn to outside.

7. Turn handle fabric as described above and topstitch. Slip ends of handle through rings sewn on duffel straps and turn under 3″ (7.6 cm). Reinforce-stitch the turned-under section as described on page 148.

Placing the straps

3″ = 7.6 cm
7″ = 17.8 cm

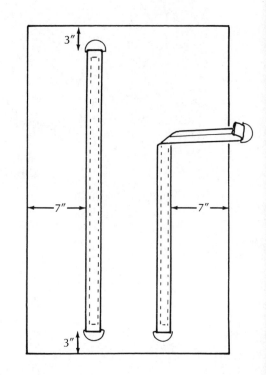

Sleeping Bag Totes

Sturdy canvas is used to construct these durable sleeping bag totes. The woven straps can be used as over-the-arm carriers, or they can be slung onto the shoulder to free the hands for other parcels. The bags work equally well as overnight totes, since they are amply proportioned to hold a complete change of clothes. A zippered pocket on the outside holds small personal items.

Make pockets according to directions on page 151. Add lettering. Both should be added before tote parts are joined. The address is printed here using stencils and permanent laundry markers. The name is added by painting with acrylic over 6″ (15.2-cm) stencils.

These sleeping bag totes are constructed in part like Basic Tote #2 (page 124). Some changes are made, however, since both ends are boxed.

1. Cut canvas tote fabric 32″ by 46″ (81.3 cm by 116.8 cm).
2. Join the short (32″ [81.3-cm]) ends with a 22″ (55.9-cm) zipper set into the middle, leaving a 5″ (12.7-cm) seam at each end of the zipper. Then fold the cylinder of fabric so that the zipper is exactly in center of one side.
3. Box ends by placing tote with zipper in center as shown in the drawing and folding in 8″ (20.3 cm) at the side. Make two 4″ (10.2-cm) pleats. This will leave front and back of tote each 14″ (35.6 cm) across. Do not sew seams to the bag. Mark or pin to indicate front and back of tote.
4. Now that front area and back area of tote are determined, plan placement of any pockets and straps.
5. Baste, then sew straps and pockets in place. Use woven strapping (from tent and awning, campers' supply, or mountaineering shop) for handles. Straps can be made to carry bag horizontally or vertically as shown in photograph.

←4″→

←14″→

Boxing the end

4″ = 10.2 cm
14″ = 35.6 cm

Bright-colored canvas makes durable totes for travel.

Reverse side of sleeping bags shows identification. Woven canvas straps are for toting bags to campsite or airline.

Reinforcing the zipper

6. Reinforce the zipper ends by cutting and sewing a 3″ by 5″ (7.6 cm by 12.7 cm) tab over the seam at the ends of the zipper. Turn under ½″ (12 mm) at both sides and at end adjacent to zipper. Stitch as shown in the drawing.

7. Turn wrong side out. Again fold in the 8″ (20.3 cm) at sides, forming two 4″ (10.2-cm) pleats. Stitch across end over the pleats. This makes a boxed corner. Turn right side out. Topstitch each corner on the outside, sewing 2 edges of a triangle as shown in the photograph.

To carry the tote horizontally, use two 56″ (142.2-cm) lengths of strapping. To carry the bag vertically, use two 88″ (223.5-cm) lengths of strapping. Stan's bag has an 11″ by 14″ (27.9 cm by 35.6 cm) zippered pocket. The other bag has a pocket 13″ by 15″ (33 cm by 38.1 cm).

12. Evening Totes

Because evening bags are always headed out to something special, they can be special. More personalized and unique bags come out in the evening, where they are expected to carry only a few items. Obviously, the books, the reports, and the thermos won't have to be toted to an evening affair, so a tiny bag that holds comb, ID, and lipstick may suffice.

Silk Evening Bag

A simple and elegant bag, in silk, is versatile enough to accompany various outfits. The metal tassel adds a jeweled finish and its weight keeps the bag closed. The over-the-shoulder handle means it can accompany its wearer to the dance floor. At the theater or concert it leaves hands free for applause,

A rich, wine-colored silk purse is kept closed by a gold-finished metal tassel.

and avoids the last-minute hassle of what to do with a purse when you give the performer a standing ovation.

The finished size is 6″ (15.2 cm) wide by 7″ (17.8 cm) high, with a 32″ (81.3-cm) handle. Follow directions for Basic Tote #3 (page 126), with the following variations:

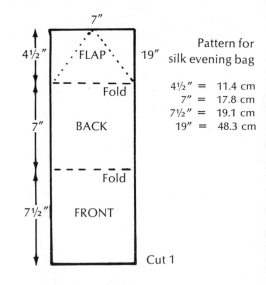

Pattern for silk evening bag

4½″ =	11.4 cm
7″ =	17.8 cm
7½″ =	19.1 cm
19″ =	48.3 cm

1. Cut bag and lining according to the pattern.
2. Cut off corners of the flap to make a triangular shape. To do this, draw a straight line from center of flap end to ½″ (12 mm) of top fold line on each side.
3. With right sides together, sew side seams of bag. Repeat for lining. Turn bag right side out. Do not turn lining.
4. With right sides together, sew flap to lining.
5. Turn and slip lining into bag. Turn top edge of bag and lining under so no raw edges show and blindstitch.
6. Add cord strap and tassel.

Mylar Makeup Tote

An evening makeup tote has a bright, two-colored exterior which opens to show a brilliant lining in the flap. The mirrored Mylar is available at

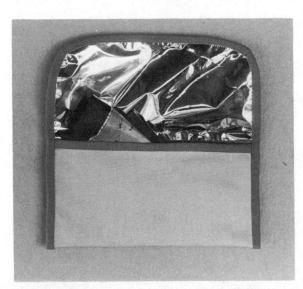

A lining of mirrored Mylar is a useful surprise in the inside of a small makeup tote.

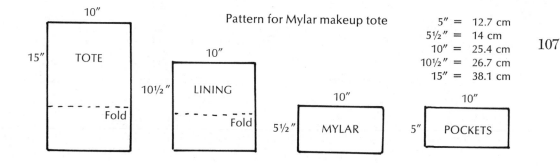

Pattern for Mylar makeup tote

5″ =	12.7 cm
5½″ =	14 cm
10″ =	25.4 cm
10½″ =	26.7 cm
15″ =	38.1 cm

hobby shops or graphic supply stores. Here, the reflective lining is cut to fit just the flap of the tote and all cut edges are bound.

While the Mylar exhibits wildly distorted images on the surface as it moves, when held still it offers enough of a mirror to get lipstick on straight.

The finished size when open is 10″ by 10″ (25.4 cm by 25.4 cm). The bag is similar to Basic Tote #3 (page 126) in appearance but it is assembled with these variations:

1. Cut tote parts according to the pattern which includes a ½″ (12-mm) seam allowance. Cut binding 1½″ by 30″ (3.8 cm by 76.2 cm) and 1½″ by 10″ (3.8 cm by 25.4 cm). Pockets and binding can be cut from same fabric as the lining if desired.
2. Fold ½″ (12 mm) of the 10″ (25.4-cm) end of lining fabric over the 10″ (25.4-cm) edge of Mylar, overlapping ½″ (12 mm). Topstitch. See the drawing.
3. Add pockets to lining if desired. To sew pockets, turn under ¼″ (6 mm) at each of the 10″ (25.4-cm) edges of the fabric. Sew one, leaving the other basted. Match stitched end with bottom of lining. Pin basted edge next to fold line of lining. Topstitch next to fold line. Then topstitch 2 vertical lines to separate the fabric into 3 pockets. Leave outside edges open.
4. Place lining fabric with Mylar over top fabric, wrong sides together. Round corners of flap, using a cup or glass as a guide.

Topstitching lining on Mylar   Topstitching binding to tote

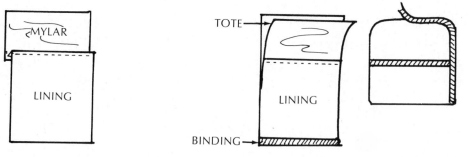

5. Place the 10″ (25.4-cm) length of binding on top of lining at straight end (next to pocket openings). Have right sides of binding and lining together. Baste, then stitch with a ½″ (12-mm) seam, being sure to catch all 3 layers (binding, lining, and tote). Fold binding to outside. Turn under ¼″ (6 mm) and baste. Then topstitch basted edge to the outside of the tote.

6. Fold bag and lining on fold line. Pin. Next pin 30″ (76.2-cm) binding strip, with right sides together, to outside of bag. Sew, easing around corner. Trim. Fold binding to inside, baste carefully, and topstitch. Sew binding in 1 long seam which covers raw edges of sides and top as shown in the drawing. Be sure that side seams catch tote, lining, and pocket ends in the binding seams. Tuck in the end of binding and hand-stitch.

Patchwork Face Bag

Fractured images result from photographic prints on fabric, cut into rectangles. They are assembled into a kind of facial patchwork with seams on the outside of the bag. Top stitching emphasizes the structure, and buttons are added at corners where the pieces meet.

All patchwork is completed before bag parts are put together. The finished size of this bag is 7″ by 7″ (17.8 cm by 17.8 cm), with a salvaged 7″ (17.8-cm) zipper, separated, used for the handle. This bag can be made according to Basic Tote #5 (page 130) if it is left unzipped.

To make this bag:

1. Finish patchwork pieces for tote front and back, making them 7″ by 7″ (17.8 cm by 17.8 cm) finished size. Add buttons and thread.
2. Insert a zipper between the top of tote front and top of tote back.
3. Use machine satin stitch to join sides and bottom at outside edge.
4. Attach ends of a separated zipper with a button sewn through both zipper parts at top to form handle.

Velveteen Evening Bag

This drawstring bag of velveteen can be carried over the wrist or tied at the waist. It is made up of two rectangular pieces of fabric cut into a half-circle at one end.

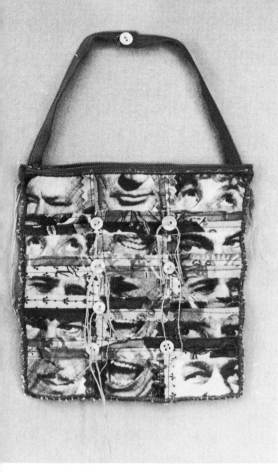

Fragmented views of face prints are pieces
in an evening bag by Sas Colby.

Drawstring pouch has a machine-appliqué design.
By Monica Malone.

The finished bag is 6″ by 8″ (15.2 cm by 20.3 cm). Follow the Basic
Tote #6 (page 131), with the following variations:

1. Cut 2 separate shapes, 7″ by 10″ (17.8 cm by 25.4 cm). Use a saucer or
   other circular shape to round the bottom ends.
2. Sew according to basic directions, leaving openings at both sides for
   drawstring.

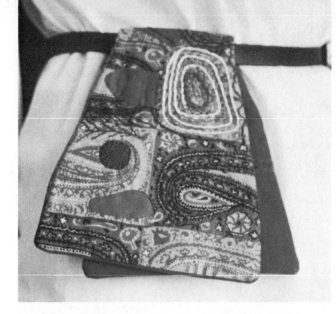

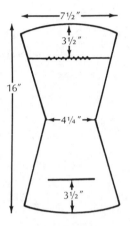

On this belted bag the zippers open to inside pockets.

Belt Tote

An embroidered evening bag hangs over a belt and frees the wearer's hands. A paisley fabric, embellished with appliqué and stitching, presents a dressy face. Or turn it around and an orange velveteen bag has a more casual, sporty look. Embroidery is worked before tote pieces are assembled. You will need a 3½" (8.9-cm) zipper. Use a doll's clothes one or cut off a plastic one.

The finished size is 15" (38.1 cm) by 6½" (16.5 cm) wide at base.

1. Cut a piece of velveteen 17" (43 cm) long and 7½" (19.1 cm) wide. Cut it across 4" (10.2 cm) from one end. Join the 2 pieces together, inserting the zipper using a ½" (12-mm) seam allowance. You will now have a 16" by 7½" (40.6 cm by 19.1 cm) piece of velveteen.
2. Make a 3" (7.6-cm) bound buttonhole 3½" (8.9 cm) from the other end.
3. Following the pattern, cut velveteen and lining material (use any paisley or print).
4. With the right sides together, join velveteen to print. Turn through buttonhole opening.
5. To close off the pockets, sew 2 lines of French knots or other decorative embroidery stitches across the bag about 3½" (8.9 cm) from the narrow center of the bag. Be sure that these stitches attach the velveteen and the print, but keep knots and any long stitches between the layers.

This long-handled denim tote was designed by Janice Rosenberg.

Denim Evening Bag

Designed to complement a long denim skirt, this tiny over-the-shoulder tote holds the evening's essentials. The casual nature of the fabric does not detract from the dressy nature of the design. Follow instructions for the silk evening bag on page 105. The patterns are identical, except the denim bag has a piping made of the lining material and it is added as the flap is sewn to the lining.

13. A Gallery of Unusual Totes

Once the basic need for totes as carryalls has been satisfied, the urge to individualize can take over. That smooth, flat expanse of material is as irresistible to fiber artists as a canvas is to a painter.

Here are examples of totes made by quilters, soft-sculpture makers, stitchers, and various fiber artists. Many may seem "beyond" our use, since some would actually require courage to be carried. It is not possible to carry some of these creations without attracting a certain amount of attention. But they open possibilities, and offer ideas that can be modified by those of us who are more hesitant or timid about wearing our art.

A few of these bags are really gallery pieces or works for exhibition. Humor runs rampant, and the puns alone justify some of the bags' existence. The arm chair or chairperson's bag (a chair-shaped bag to be hung over one arm) and the shoulder bag (shoulders included in the bag!) are just two of many examples.

This gallery of bags, then, is for amusement and inspiration. You may not do anything similar as a first bag, but later you'll come back to them, since these are inventive, ingenious, and exhibit a fine sense of craftsmanship. Perhaps your first unusual additions or personalized versions will be limited to what you add on the inside of the tote, or under the flap . . . surprises for the wearer. One woman, new to tote design, embroidered a favorite quotation under the shoulder strap of her bag. Later, as courage develops, you'll be willing to share your humor and comments with those around you. Even strangers!

Doggy Bag

A leather dog leash was appropriated for the shoulder strap of this tote. The mouth opens wide and provides access to the innermost recesses. The

White vinyl teeth line the
opening of this leather doggy bag
by designer Peggy Moulton.

leather pouchlike bag consists basically of two large triangles, with the top folded down to make the dog's head. The construction is similar to that of the flat bag, as in Basic Tote #5 (page 130). The finished size is 12″ by 13½″ (30.5 cm by 34.3 cm) with mouth closed.

Bicycle Tote

Totes need not all be fabric. Here is one of wood which has a box for a base. Calligrapher Marilyn Judson has applied wood letters over the

Words, words, words,
all cut from hardwood
with a jigsaw,
glorify this wood tote
which clamps to a
bicycle rack.

surface using glue to hold the wood veneer words in place. The words reflect the box's use—notes, pens, papers, books, lunch, and glasses. A metal clamp holds the box to the bike's rack. It can then be removed and carried, like a briefcase, to office or school.

Labeled Levi's

Dozens of clothing labels were stitched to denim to make this glorious tote. Using an old pair of blue jeans as the basic shape, the designer inserted a lining that provides the bag or container. The legs are left open. Waistline of the discarded denim pants forms the top edge of the tote, and a strap is added at the sides. The strap is covered with labels, also stitched in place with heavy embroidery and satin stitch.

Sunday-Go-to-Meetin'

This unusual tote is made up from 21 blocks of the Cathedral Window quilt pattern. Four of the cut and turned petal shapes of the pattern have been eliminated from the center of one tote side to add the embroidery and appliqué.

Denim patches, 9″ (22.9 cm) square, provide the bases. Each block finishes at 4″ (10.2 cm) square, making a tote 12″ (30.5 cm) square. Three blocks form the handle, making it 4″ by 12″ (10.2 cm by 30.5 cm) finished size (from top of bag on one side to top of bag on the other).

As the Cathedral Window blocks are joined, the colored-print fabrics

Any teenager would revel in the use of
this colorful blue jeans bag made by artist
Peggy Moulton for her daughter.

Cathedral Window quilt blocks add color
and texture to Wanda Hottle's tote.

are inserted to cover the seams. The denim is then rolled and stitched to
conceal raw edges of the print. Blocks are placed 3 across and 6 down for
the entire purse, with 3 added in a row at one end to form the handle.
Side seams are sewn and the open end of the handle is hand-stitched to the
other side of the bag.

Hand and machine stitching over padded cotton fabric quilt the surface of this bag. Fine threads with beads hang streamer-like from the surface.

Woman's Bag

Sas Colby combines drawing with stitchery. Her sewing machine becomes a drawing tool as she superimposes the linear pattern over a floral-print cotton sateen. The binding and spaghetti strap handle are made from printed materials. The bag is made according to Basic Tote #5 (page 130).

The two petal shapes were cut and decorated with machine-stitched embroidery, over padded fabric, before any parts were joined. The top figure, padded and stitched, was made separately and stitched to the inside of the bag. It is finished on both facing and back sides, and the hands extend over the front of the bag to hold tops together with a snap.

Carpetbag

Woven in one piece, this bag was shaped as the fabric was made. It is tapestry weave on a warp of wool and synthetic, using thick, handspun yarns along with blends of wool and Orlon . . . all dyed with procion dyes.

The weaving was then folded in half to form the bag. Side seams are Cretan-stitched together or slip-woven with a needle. Embroidery-hoop handles were sewn to the top sections. The bag was lined with cotton fabric and the seam where the woven material overlapped the ring was covered with the lining.

Pockets were woven separately and added. The flower is tucked into one of the open pockets.

Woven Jute Tote

This unusual tote will be of interest to hand weavers. It was made with a triangular weave on a 36″ (91.4-cm) frame. The parts were woven to finish the same size as the triangles needed for Basic Tote #9 (page 138).

The jute used in this bag adds stiffness and durability. There is a fold at the bottom of the bag, and warp ends form a fringe at the sides. The plaids of this tote are matched, and since the bias edge is woven, it is finished and does not require hemming or lining. This somewhat complex weaving process was accomplished by Eleanor Van De Water who learned triangular weaving from the well-known hand weaver, Jean Wilson.

Tapestry weave was used in this tote, woven to shape with hand-dyed yarns. By Bucky King.

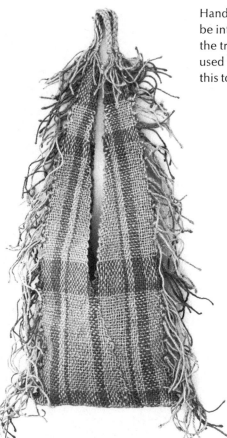

Hand weavers will be intrigued by the triangular weave used to construct this tote.

Shoulder Bag

Peggy Moulton's sense of the ridiculous couldn't resist the idea of a "shoulder bag." Here, the he-man's shoulders are made of naugahyde richly embellished with tattoos and embroidered hair. The gold expansion band of the wristwatch provides a closure. It is secured to the bag and the hand can be slipped out and lifted up, revealing the expansive interior of the tote.

The tank shirt fits not only over the broad tanned shoulders of the bag but over the wearer's shoulder (or forearm) as well. The intricate patchwork of the bag is heavily stitched by machine sewing to provide an overall pattern and texture.

The structure of the tank shirt portion of this tote is a variation of Basic Tote #4 (page 128). The bottom corners have been softened and rounded and an extension of the front and back panels form the straps. The finished size is 14″ (35.6 cm) wide, 23″ (58.4 cm) high, and 5″ (12.7 cm) deep.

More conversation piece than shopping bag, this witty and inventive tote becomes a walking exhibition of the artist's work.

Needleweaving technique allows for a free-flowing form in this richly colored, very textural bag.

Designer Kay Aronson has her tongue in her cheek (and her hand in the elephant's foot).

Elephantote

Luxuriously textured in velvets, handspun yarns, wrapped cords, and feathers, this bag is shaped like an elephant's foot. Appliquéd forms at the bottom suggest the toes. Perhaps it could carry peanuts to the zoo. The handsome appliqué and embroidery make it appear complex, while the design is basically a very simple one. It is an elaboration of Basic Tote #4 (page 128), and measures 14½" (36.8 cm) wide by 16" (40.6 cm) high, with a 16" (40.6-cm) handle extending above top of tote.

Needleweaving Tote

Referred to variously as needleweaving or detached buttonhole, a single stitch is used to make this highly textured, inviting bag. Using the stitch in a manner like freehand drawing, the designer, Betty Auchard, has let the pattern evolve, changing colors and textures as she felt they would enhance the design.

A wildly textured bag invites
handling and belies the simplicity
of its basic structure.

Security Bag

Combining the qualities of elegance and ragamuffin, this piece is referred to as a "security bag" by its designer. Tufts of fur, buttons, and small
pennant shapes give the wearer objects to hold on to.

Doris Hoover made up the textured panel using crumpled velours,
smooth velveteens, fur, and corduroy. Buttons were added for textural

Buttons, used decoratively,
add hard-edge contrast to the soft
furs and velvets.

contrast and pattern. The panel was then used as one section of Basic Tote #4 (page 128). Pennants were hand-sewn to the lower edge after the bag was assembled.

Binding at the top edge secures the bag to the lining, and matching binding edges the strap. The button and tab at the top provide a closure.

Chairperson Bag

Only a sense of humor like Ann de Witt's could have come up with an "arm chair" like this one.

The bag part is really very usable. The construction consists of a square bag over which a flap (the chair seat) falls. The shoulder strap has been elaborated to suggest the chair back. A coin purse, sewn to the flap, opens to hold change or keys. The finished size is 14″ by 26″ (35.6 cm by 66 cm).

The whimsical concept of this bag doesn't overshadow its underlying usefulness. It isn't just a jest from Ann de Witt.

14. The Basic Totes

Almost all the totes in this book are made according to the basic patterns in this chapter. In making any of these totes, read all the way through the directions before cutting fabric or beginning assembly. For some of these totes, lining is essential; in others it is optional. Each basic tote pattern indicates whether or not lining is required. Turn or stitch the handles according to the weight of the fabric.

NOTE:

Cut size always refers to the cut pattern size, including the seams. Fold lines are indicated on the pattern piece.

Finished size always refers to the completed measurement of the tote. If the tote is boxed, the measurement is made for one facing side only and does not include the side panel. For handles, finished size refers to the measurement from the top of the bag at one end to the top of the bag at the other end. It does not include the overlap.

Depth refers to distance from front to back in a boxed or shaped tote. Some totes, such as the envelope type, have no depth measurement.

BASIC TOTE #1 — Side Inset Tote

Simply constructed from just three pattern pieces, this tote has a boxed effect when finished. The boxing gives the bag form and adds roominess. Variations of this pattern are limitless, since changing the proportions is a simple matter. By using contrasting colors on the sides, bags take on an entirely new and different look. For a crisp, tailored look, use a stiff material such as ticking or duck. A soft fabric, like velveteen, gives a casual or crushed look.

The velveteen tote, book tote, and all-day bag are all variations of the same pattern from Basic Tote #1.

This pattern is one of the most popular for totes and is shown frequently throughout this book.

The finished size of this tote is 14″ (35.5 cm) wide, 14″ (35.5 cm) high, and 5″ (12.7 cm) deep. The handle is 1″ by 15″ (2.5 cm by 38.1 cm).

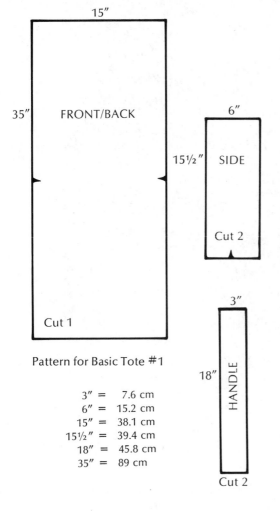

15″

35″   FRONT/BACK

Cut 1

Pattern for Basic Tote #1

3″	=	7.6 cm
6″	=	15.2 cm
15″	=	38.1 cm
15½″	=	39.4 cm
18″	=	45.8 cm
35″	=	89 cm

6″

15½″   SIDE

Cut 2

3″

18″   HANDLE

Cut 2

1. Cut the pattern pieces and mark the notches. The pattern includes a ½″ (12-mm) seam allowance. The lining is optional.
2. With right sides together, pin and baste the side pieces to the long front/back panel, matching notches at center bottom. Clip at corners. Machine-stitch, then turn right side out.
3. Fold top edge of bag to inside ¼″ (6 mm) and machine-stitch.
4. Line if desired by cutting and sewing lining material the same as the tote, but do not turn. Omit step 3. Trim ½″ (12 mm) off top edge of lining and slip into place in the tote so that the finished side of the lining forms inside of bag.
5. Baste lining to tote at top edges. Turn lining and bag top down 1″ (2.5 cm), press and baste.
6. Make handles and attach to inside of bag according to directions beginning on page 146.
7. Topstitch ¾″ (18 mm) from folded top edge, stitching handles in place with top stitching.
8. Tack handles to bag at outside top edge to keep them in place. This is optional.

VARIATION

If you wish to add pockets, sew them to the tote fabric or the lining fabric after fabric is cut but before parts are joined.

BASIC TOTE #2 — One-Piece Boxed Tote

Fold a piece of cloth through the center, sew up the sides, and you have made a bag in the easiest possible way. An additional seam at the

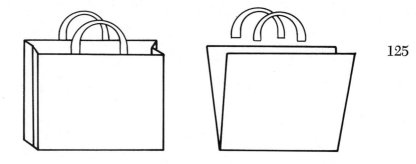

corners boxes the base and gives it shape. From that point on, the addition of flaps, straps, handles, or pockets offers personalized variations.

The finished size of the tote is 16″ (40.64 cm) wide, 13½″ (34.29 cm) high, and 5″ (12.7 cm) deep. The handle is 1½″ by 16″ (3.8 cm by 40.64 cm). The measurement from side seam to side seam is 21″ (53.34 cm), but boxing makes the front area 16″ (40.64 cm).

1. Cut tote and handles (lining is optional) according to the pattern which includes a ½″ (12-mm) seam allowance.
2. Fold fabric on the fold line with right sides together. Stitch the side seams.
3. To box the corners, place side seam directly on top of the fold line, as in the drawing. Stitch across as shown. Repeat the boxing process for the other corner. Since this makes a right-angle triangle at the corner, the sewn line is always twice as long as the distance from the point of the folded corner to the seam line. The stitched corner can be either wider or narrower than the one shown, according to preference or need. If, for example, the stitched line is 4″ (10.16 cm) across, it is sewn exactly 2″ (5.08 cm) from the point. This would make a bag that was 4″ (10.16 cm) wide at the base. Then turn.

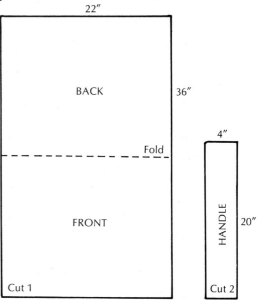

Pattern for Basic Tote #2

4″ = 10.2 cm
20″ = 50.8 cm
22″ = 55.9 cm
36″ = 91.4 cm

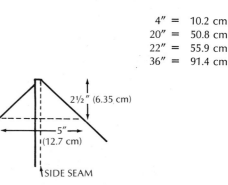

Boxing the corners

4. Fold ½″ (12 mm) of the top edge to the inside of the tote and machine-stitch.

5. If bag is to be lined, repeat the above process for lining except for turning and step 4. Then slip lining in place inside the bag. Stiff fabrics may not require any lining.

6. Fold over 1½″ (3.8 cm) of the top edge of the tote material over the lining or onto itself if no lining is used. Trim lining as necessary, being sure that the stitched edge of the tote covers raw edges of the lining. Baste. Topstitch.

VARIATION

If pockets are to be added, they are sewn to the outside fabric or the lining fabric after those pieces are cut but before the parts are joined.

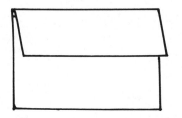

BASIC TOTE #3 — Envelope Bag

The envelope tote is made, as the name suggests, like a paper envelope with or without a flap. A single piece of cloth is folded and sewn at the sides and endless variations may be devised.

The finished size of the tote flap is 3½″ by 8″ (8.9 cm by 20.3 cm), and tote, 5½″ by 8″ (14 cm by 20.3 cm).

1. Cut tote and lining according to pattern which includes ½″ (12-mm) seam allowance. If inside pockets are desired, sew them to the lining fabric according to directions on page 151.

2. Sew lining to tote with right sides together, leaving an opening at flap end for turning.

3. Turn right side out and fold under seam allowance at opening. Press.

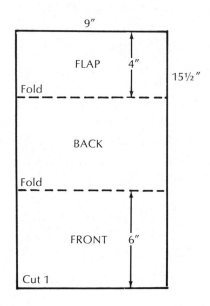

Pattern for Basic Tote #3

4″ =	10.2 cm
6″ =	15.2 cm
9″ =	22.9 cm
15½″ =	39.4 cm

4. Measure 5½″ (14 cm) from one end and fold front over back with lining to inside. Pin or baste. Topstitch one side, around the flap, and down the other side, making 1 continuous line of stitching.

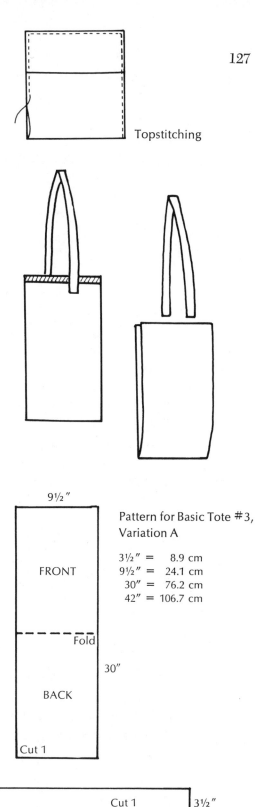

Topstitching

VARIATION A

The lining of this tote forms a binding at the top so choose a complementary lining color.

The finished size is 15″ by 8½″ (38.1 cm by 21.6 cm). The length of the strap from top edge to top edge is 38″ (96.5 cm).

1. Cut tote and lining according to pattern which includes ½″ (12-mm) seam allowance.
2. Fold tote fabric in half with right sides together as in the drawing and stitch side seams. Repeat for lining.
3. Turn tote right side out and slip lining into it. Trim tote as necessary so that lining extends 1″ (2.5 cm) above top of tote.
4. Fold lining over top raw edge of tote to the outside. Turn edge under ½″ (12 mm) and baste.
5. Topstitch lining to outside of tote.
6. Sew strap as instructed on page 146. Finish ends.
7. Pin handles on outside of bag at center top of each side with handle extending down 1½″ (3.8 cm) from top edge.
8. Attach handle to bag as instructed on page 148.

9½″

FRONT

Fold

30″

BACK

Cut 1

Pattern for Basic Tote #3, Variation A

3½″ = 8.9 cm
9½″ = 24.1 cm
30″ = 76.2 cm
42″ = 106.7 cm

42″

HANDLE   Cut 1   3½″

VARIATION B

The finished size is 14″ wide by 11″ high (35.6 cm by 27.9 cm), with an 11″ (27.9-cm) handle.

1. Cut tote and lining according to the pattern which includes ½″ (12-mm) seam allowance.
2. Add continuous pockets to lining according to personal preference. Follow directions on page 152. Be sure top edge of pocket is at least 3″ (7.6 cm) from top edge of lining, since top of bag will be folded over to the inside.
3. Fold tote in half with right sides together and stitch side seams. Repeat for lining.
4. Turn tote right side out. Turn under ½″ (12 mm) of raw edge to inside and topstitch.
5. Insert lining and trim lining to fit just under the line of top stitching. Baste together.
6. Fold tote top over 2″ (5.1 cm) to inside of bag. Pin, baste, then topstitch so that the tote fabric covers raw edge of lining.
7. Cut handles according to the drawing. Fold, sew long edge, and turn.
8. Attach handles to outside of tote according to directions on page 148.

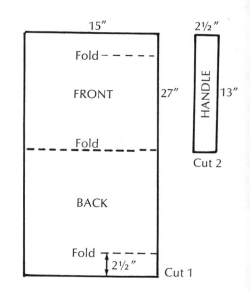

Pattern for Basic Tote #3, Variation B

2½″	=	6.4 cm
13″	=	33 cm
15″	=	38.1 cm
27″	=	68.6 cm

BASIC TOTE #4 — Boxed Bag

This boxed bag, which has a very tailored air about it, consists of three pattern pieces. It is one of the most versatile patterns, suitable for any fabric that has some body or stiffness. Canvas, ticking, leather, and upholstery fabrics are especially well suited.

These drawstring totes have a seemingly unlimited capacity for beach gear. (Photo by Jean Ray Laury)

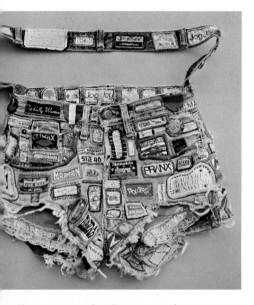

Corduroy, fur, and velvet invite the touch in this bag by Doris Hoover. (Photo by Gayle Smalley)

Cutoff Levi's completely patterned with clothing labels make an ample tote. ...designer Peggy Moulton. (Photo by Stan Bitters)

Totes carry sleeping bags,
a change of clothes,
and travel necessities.
(Photo by Jean Ray Laury)

An assortment of bags showing just how versatile totes can be. (Photo by Jean Ray Laury)

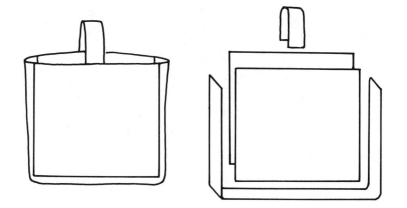

The finished size is 13″ (33 cm) high, 12½″ (31.8 cm) wide, and 3½″ (8.9 cm) deep. The handle from top edge of tote to opposite top edge is 11″ (27.9 cm).

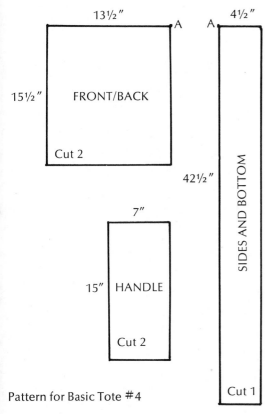

Pattern for Basic Tote #4

4½″ =	11.4 cm
7″ =	17.8 cm
13½″ =	34.3 cm
15″ =	38.1 cm
15½″ =	39.4 cm
42½″ =	108 cm

1. Cut tote pieces as shown in the pattern which includes ½″ (12-mm) seam allowance on all edges.
2. With right sides together, sew long side strip to front of tote, matching the A's. Continue down side, across bottom, and up other side. Ease at corners, clipping as necessary. Repeat for the back of tote. Turn right side out.
3. If lining is used, sew it the same way as the tote but do not turn and slip it inside of the tote so that finished seams form inside.
4. Fold over ½″ (12 mm) of the top edge of tote to the inside of the bag. Topstitch. Then fold 1½″ (3.8 cm) of the top to the inside of the bag. Press. If lining is used, trim top edge of lining to fit. Let top fold of tote cover the raw edge of the lining. Topstitch.
5. Make and add single handle across top opening as indicated following directions beginning on page 146.

VARIATION A

For shoulder bag, lengthen handle and add so that it becomes an extension of the side panel.

VARIATION B

If pockets are desired, either inside or outside, sew them to the cut fabric before parts are joined.

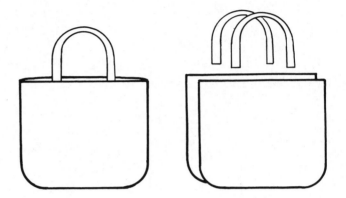

BASIC TOTE #5 — Flat Tote

Two pieces of fabric, cut identically, can be sewn together to form a bag. Because the pieces are not folded, the outside form is not limited to a rectangular shape. This pattern adapts easily to all shapes—half circles, ovals, or triangles as well as squares.

The finished size is 13″ (33 cm) wide by 11″ (27.9 cm) high, with 15″ (38.1-cm) handles.

1. Cut tote and handles (lining optional) according to the patterns which allow ½″ (12-mm) seam allowance.
2. Use a plate or saucer as a guide to curve the bottom corners.
3. With right sides facing, join front and back pieces. Leave top edge open. Turn.

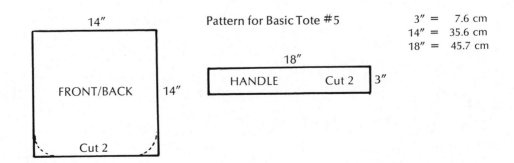

14″

FRONT/BACK · 14″

Cut 2

Pattern for Basic Tote #5

18″

HANDLE · Cut 2 · 3″

3″ = 7.6 cm
14″ = 35.6 cm
18″ = 45.7 cm

4. Repeat if lining is to be used, but don't turn. Trim top edge of lining ½″ (12 mm). Slip into tote and baste at top of lining edge.

5. Turn under top edge of tote fabric ½″ (12 mm) and machine-stitch.

6. Fold 2″ (5.1 cm) of the top edge of tote to the inside and topstitch in place. This fold should cover the raw top edge of lining.

7. Sew handles.

8. Attach handles to tote (see page 147).

BASIC TOTE #6 — Drawstring Tote

The pouch or drawstring bag is found throughout the world and has been known for centuries. Its shape is simple and the cord that closes the bag doubles as the handle. It has a flexibility not found in all totes, so that bulky, lumpy, or odd-shaped objects can easily be accommodated.

This simple and extremely versatile drawstring bag is made from a single flat piece of material. The proportions can vary endlessly, but here is one basic pattern. The finished size is 10″ (25.4 cm) wide by 12″ (30.5 cm) high, with a 36″ (91.4-cm) cord.

1. Cut 1 piece according to pattern which includes ½″ (12-mm) seam allowance.

2. Fold over top edge ½″ (12 mm) to inside and stitch. Fold tote at center line, stitch bottom and side seams. Leave the top 3″ (7.6 cm) of the side seam open as in the drawing.

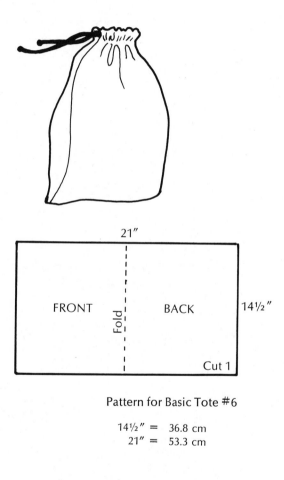

Pattern for Basic Tote #6

14½″ = 36.8 cm
21″ = 53.3 cm

Stitching bottom and side seams

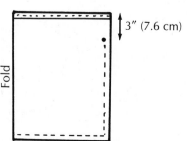

3″ (7.6 cm)

3. Press side seam open to lie flat.

4. Topstitch the sides and bottom of the 3″ (7.6-cm) opening, as shown in the drawing.

5. Turn 1½″ (3.8 cm) of the top edge to the inside, and topstitch to bag, as in the drawing. Run cord through open channel. For materials suitable for drawstrings, see page 149. A large safety pin attached to one end of the drawstring will help in putting it through the channel.

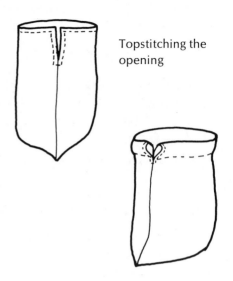

Topstitching the opening

Topstitching to form the channel

VARIATION A

This variation works best with a solid color, since the reverse side of the fabric shows as the top band. Follow basic instructions but sew side seam to within 1″ (2.5 cm) of top. Turn right sides out. Then fold over ¼″ (6 mm) of top raw edge to outside. Stitch. Fold over another 1″ (2.5 cm) to outside, topstitch in place as in the drawing. Run cord through open channel.

VARIATION B

Make bag from 2 rectangles, each 14″ (35.6 cm) by 11″ (27.9 cm). Assemble like basic drawstring bag, leaving 3″ (7.6 cm) open at top seam on each side. Use 2 drawstrings, 1 coming out each side.

VARIATION C

Follow the instructions for Basic Tote #6 but cut an additional fabric band of contrasting color 21″ by 3″ (53.3 cm by 7.6 cm). Turn under and stitch ½″ (12 mm) at each of the 3″ (7.6-cm) ends. Join tote bottom and side seams, sewing all the way to the top of the sides. Press side seam open. With right side of band to inside of the tote top, stitch together, matching side seams. Fold band to outside of tote, turn a ½″ (12-mm) hem, and baste. Then topstitch band to bag, leaving an opening at the seam for drawstring as in the drawing. The same method of adding a channel can be used when 2 rectangles of fabric make up the tote as described in Variation B, which requires 2 drawstrings.

VARIATION D

Follow basic tote directions but fold over a 3″ (7.6-cm) hem to inside at top edge of tote. Baste and sew. Then machine-stitch a separate channel in the hem for drawstring as shown in the drawing.

VARIATION E

Join 2 or more different colors of fabric in horizontal bands to make desired tote shape. Assemble according to basic pattern, using any of the methods described to make a channel for the cord.

VARIATION F

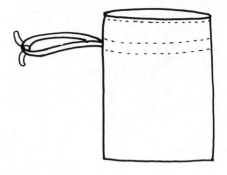

Cut basic drawstring tote and sew bottom and side seams. Repeat for lining. Turn under ½″ (12 mm) at top raw edge of tote and press. Repeat for lining. Slip lining inside tote, matching hems. Baste and topstitch. Sew 1 single line of stitching 2″ (5.1 cm) from top of bag. Sew another 1″ (2.5 cm) below the first one. Open side seam of tote between lines of stitching and run drawstring through the opening.

BASIC TOTE #7 — Cylinders

The cylinder provides a simple and universal container form which can be used for a tote. It can be varied in size and proportion so that essentially a thimble, bucket, or map tube are all cylindrical containers, and all can be adapted to fabric.

A tote bag based on the cylinder has only two pattern pieces so the principle of construction is simple. Some of those shown in this book are made entirely of fabric and have quilting, patchwork, or other decorative work applied to the surface. Others are sewn over ready-made cylinders such as oatmeal boxes, ice-cream cartons, or plastic jugs. Any of these ready-made containers can be cut down to the desired height. With a cylinder form the work is simplified, since it is possible to trace the circle used for the base from the bottom of the container and the fabric can be wrapped around the cylinder to determine the size of the vertical fabric panel.

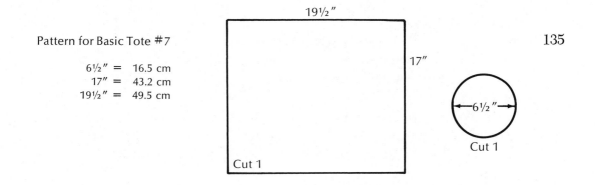

19½″

17″

6½″ = 16.5 cm
17″ = 43.2 cm
19½″ = 49.5 cm

Cut 1

←6½″→

Cut 1

The finished size is 5½″ (14 cm) wide by 16″ (40.6 cm) high, with 36″ (91.4-cm) drawstrings.

NOTE ON FABRIC TO BE USED:

If this tote is made from fabric only, without a cylindrical box used inside, some stiffening may be required if the bag is to stand upright by itself. Quilting adds body, as does appliqué or decorative surface treatments which tend to stiffen the material. A heavy canvas or duck may be adequately stiff, depending upon how large the bag is made. Lining material helps add body, and iron-on interfacings will certainly make the fabric more rigid. You may prefer a soft, floppy tote. For very soft bags, a disk may be used at the base of the tote, inserted between tote and lining. A plywood or cardboard disk can be used, or a plastic coffee can lid provides a ready-made lightweight disk. Use fabric glue to attach the base to the disk. Plastic disks can be attached with a few stitches.

1. Cut tote pieces by the pattern. This pattern fits a two-pound, ten-ounce oatmeal box (the large size). To determine the pattern for another size, find some cylinder to use as a guide. (Canister, coffee can, straight-sided wastebasket, etc.) Trace the bottom circle and add a ½″ (12-mm) seam allowance. Then measure around the cylinder on the straight side, adding a ½″ (12-mm) seam allowance at both ends of the width for the side seam. The tote material must be cut so that it extends a minimum of 6″ (15.2 cm) above the cylinder being covered.
2. Cut the same pattern pieces for lining.
3. With right sides of tote fabric together, sew side seam and do not turn.
4. With right sides together, pin bottom circle to the tote panel, easing as necessary. Baste and sew, and turn right side out.
5. Turn the top edge of tote fabric under ½″ (12 mm) and press.

6. Repeat for lining, making seams a little deeper (about ¾″ [18-mm] seams) so that lining will fit smoothly inside the box, but do not turn.

7. Put box into tote and lining into box.

8. Bring top edges of tote and lining together with turned edges meeting. Baste. Then topstitch tote and lining together.

9. Make a channel for the drawstring top by sewing 2 parallel lines of stitching, the first 1½″ (3.8 cm) from the top, the second 1″ (2.5 cm) lower. Open the side seam between those lines of stitching and insert the drawstring. A large safety pin attached to one end of the drawstring will help in putting it through the channel. For variations on the draw-string top, see Basic Tote #6 (page 131). For materials suitable for drawstrings, see page 149.

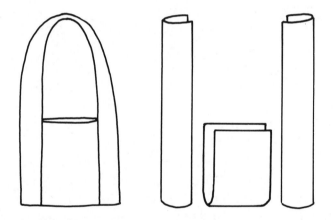

BASIC TOTE #8 — Three-Piece Shoulder Tote

Here is a tote pattern that avoids wasting *any* fabric. It is cut from a square of cloth leaving no scraps nor leftovers. The construction is simple and the resulting bag is roomy and comfortable to carry. An added extra is that the bag is reversible.

Any decorative work can be applied to the center panel before the parts are assembled. To make the bag of two colors so that the side panels contrast with the center panel, use two squares of fabric, one for the tote and one for the lining. Then alternate the two colors.

The finished size of this tote is 13″ (33 cm) by 13″ (33 cm), with handle 22″ (55.9 cm) above top of bag.

1. Cut tote and lining according to the pattern which includes a ½″ (12-mm) seam allowance.

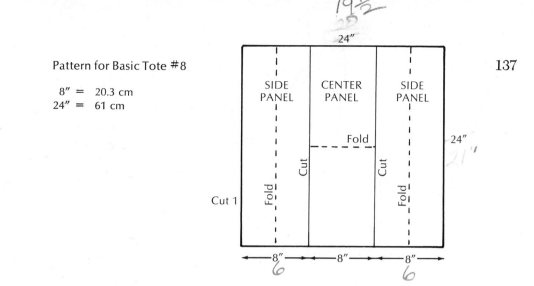

Pattern for Basic Tote #8

8" = 20.3 cm
24" = 61 cm

Cut 1

2. Fold center panel in half where shown in pattern, wrong sides facing. Fold side panels in half lengthwise, where shown, right sides facing.

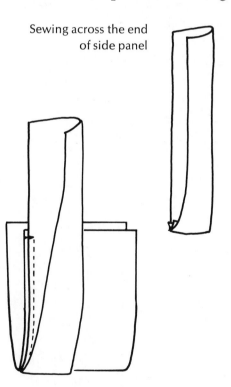

Sewing across the end of side panel

Sewing a side panel to the center panel

3. With right sides together, sew across one end of each side panel as in the drawing. Turn to outside.

4. With right sides together, sew 1 side panel to center panel, matching the side panel seam with fold of center panel. Leave ½" (12 mm) open at top edge of center section for turnover. Clip seam at that point as shown in the drawing. Press side seams toward center panel. Repeat for other side.

5. Repeat for lining.

6. With right sides together, sew lining handle and bag top to tote handle and top. Leave top end of handle open for turning.

7. Turn, slip lining into bag, and press.

8. With right sides facing, sew ends of tote handle together, leaving lining open. Turn and press.

9. Fold seam allowance under on the lining of the handle ends and blind-stitch to tote.

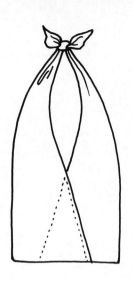

Pattern for Basic Tote #9

18" = 45.7 cm
36" = 91.4 cm

18"

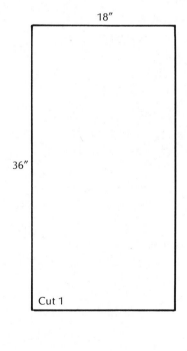

36"

Cut 1

BASIC TOTE #9
— Triangular Tie Tote

Ann de Witt devised this ingenious tote. One of the great assets of this design is that it, like Basic Tote #8, makes complete use of all the fabric, with no waste nor scraps. In addition it is comfortable and easily adjustable.

The finished size, when tied, is 11½" (29.2 cm) wide by 27" (68.6 cm) long.

1. Cut tote according to pattern which includes ½" (12-mm) seam allowance.
2. With right sides facing, sew the 36" (91.4-cm) sides together to form a tube. Finish this seam with binding or other seam finish, as it will show on the inside of the unlined bag.
3. Turn right side out and lay flat so that the seam is equidistant from the folded sides as in the drawing.

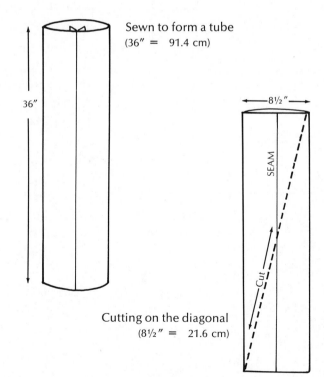

Sewn to form a tube
(36" = 91.4 cm)

36"

8½"

SEAM

Cut

Cutting on the diagonal
(8½" = 21.6 cm)

Sewing interlocking
pieces (9″ = 22.9 cm)

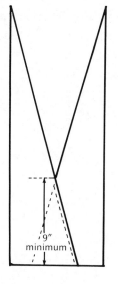

9″
minimum

4. With a yardstick or straight edge, mark a diagonal line from top to bottom of bag. Cut, making 2 triangles of equal size. Finish cut diagonal edges with binding tape.
5. Place triangles to interlock so that depth of bag is at least 9″ (22.9 cm) where triangles intersect, as shown in the drawing. Topstitch or hand-sew overlapping areas as indicated by broken lines.
6. Turn tote inside out and sew bottom seam.
7. Turn to right side. Tie knot in handle ends to form shoulder strap.

BASIC TOTE #10 — One-Piece Tote

There are a few simple totes that can be made without cutting any fabric pieces at all. These are simple but ingenious and require little time to make. Four one-piece totes are given here. The first is a stitched scarf, the next two totes utilize zippers, and the last is an unstitched square of cloth. The designs of the zippered bags are of Japanese origin and have the advantage, like the hobo tote, of opening to a flat cloth. That way they serve a dual purpose—for example, as a lunch tote which opens to become a tablecloth, or a toy tote which opens to provide a covered play area.

VARIATION A — SCARF TOTE

1. Cut 1 tote panel according to the pattern, or use a long, ready-made scarf of that proportion.

Pattern for Basic Tote #10, Variation A

15″ = 38.1 cm
45″ = 114.3 cm

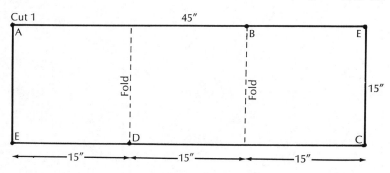

Cut 1

45″

A   B   E

Fold   Fold

15″

E   D   C

←—15″—→ ←—15″—→ ←—15″—→

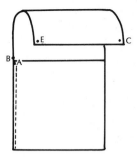

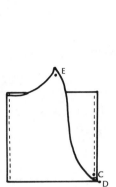

Sewing A to B

Sewing C to D

2. Finish edges by hemming or binding if cut fabric is selected.
3. Fold one end of fabric on fold line as shown, folding point A to point B. Sew together as close to the edge as possible as in the drawing.
4. Fold the other end on fold line matching C to D. Sew as close to the edge as possible.
5. Corners are left loose. Pull both E corners out and tie to form a handle.

VARIATION B — ZIPPERED TOTE

1. Use 1 yard of fabric, or a 36" (91.4-cm) square. Hem or finish all 4 edges, or line with a second square of fabric.
2. Use 4 zippers, 18" (45.7 cm) long, in either matching or contrasting colors. Locate center of fabric by folding it on the diagonal as shown. Place zippers on right side of fabric as shown in the drawing and open

Pattern for Basic Tote #10, Variation B

6"	=	15.2 cm	18"	=	45.7 cm
11"	=	27.9 cm	36"	=	91.4 cm

Laying out the zippers for Variation B.

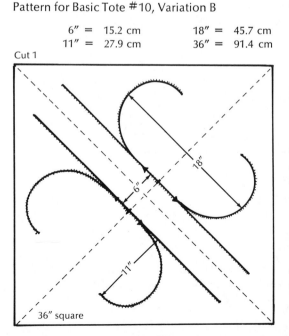

Cut 1

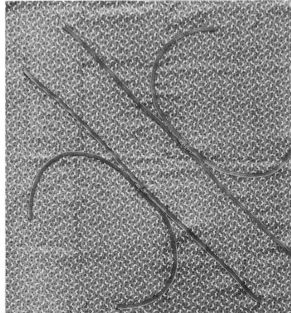

zippers beyond the first 3½″ (8.9 cm). Sew the straight lines of zippers first, making sure that the zippers are parallel to one another and closed ends touch.

3. Mark with tailor's chalk the line where the second side of the zipper is to be sewn. Stitch in place.

4. Close zippers to form tote, and use corners to make handles.

VARIATION C — ZIPPERED TOTE

1. Construction for this tote is the same as for the zippered tote of Variation B above, but zippers are placed according to the pattern for Variation C.

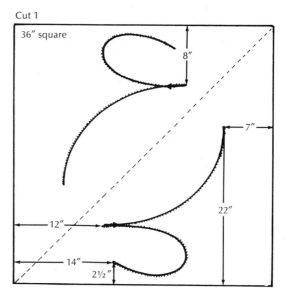

Cut 1

36″ square

8″

7″

22″

12″

14″

2½″

Pattern for Basic Tote #10, Variation C

2½″ =	6.4 cm	14″ =	35.6 cm
7″ =	17.8 cm	22″ =	55.9 cm
8″ =	20.3 cm	36″ =	91.4 cm
12″ =	30.5 cm		

VARIATION D — HOBO TOTE

1. Cut a square of fabric for the hobo bag. A 36″ (91.4-cm) square works well and utilizes a full yard of fabric, though any size square can be used.

2. Hem and finish edges or line the square with another piece of fabric.

3. The fabric is wrapped around the contents so that the four corners come together at the top. Diagonally opposed corners are tied together to make the bag.

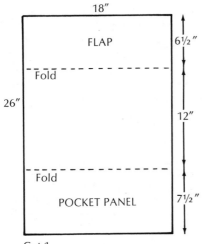

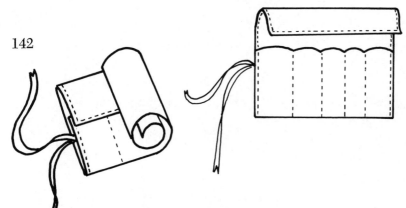

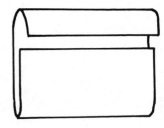

BASIC TOTE #11 — Roll-up Tote

Carrying a collection of small items—sewing tools, car tools, bottles, or drawing pens—often requires a special kind of tote which will keep the individual pieces separate. The roll-up tote does just that. It is similar to cloths made for silverware in which compartments contain single objects. A flap at the top keeps things from sliding out, and rolling them all into a tube shape offers a compact package for travel.

The finished size of the tote is 12″ (30.5 cm) high by 17″ (43.2 cm) wide. Pockets are 7″ by 17″ (17.8 cm by 43.2 cm), and flap is 6″ by 17″ (15.2 cm by 43.2 cm). One yard of ribbon is used for the tie.

	18″
	FLAP
	Fold
26″	
	POCKET PANEL
	Cut 1

6½″ (top flap section)
12″
7½″ (pocket panel section)

Pattern for Basic Tote #11

6½″ =	16.5 cm	18″ =	45.7 cm
7½″ =	19.1 cm	26″ =	66 cm
12″ =	30.5 cm		

1. Cut tote and lining according to pattern which includes ½″ (12-mm) seam allowance.
2. With right sides together, machine-stitch all edges of tote to lining, leaving a 4″ (10.2-cm) opening on one side for turning.
3. Turn right side out and close the opening with blind stitching. Topstitch on all four sides.
4. Fold pocket section up on fold line with linings facing. Insert ribbon or cord in this fold at one of the side seams, and baste the side seam. Topstitch.
5. Topstitch vertical lines to produce pockets of desired widths for the specific tools to be carried.

BASIC TOTE #12 — Covered Box Tote

Cardboard boxes, covered with fabric, make versatile totes where a rigid form is needed. Some boxes may be finished with a slipcover approach. Others, especially where heavier fabrics are used, can be finished entirely with flexible fabric glue.

A middle-weight or sturdy fabric should be used, since fabric glue will soak through a fine material. Upholstery fabric, corduroy, duck, or canvas all work well.

TO LINE THE BOX:

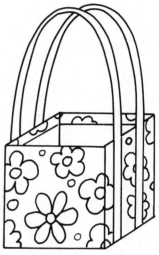

1. Choose a box that is appropriate in size for your specific tote needs. The one shown in the drawing is 8″ (20.3 cm) square.

2. To line inside of box, measure the inside depth and the distance around the inside of the box. Add 1″ (2.5 cm) to both depth and length measurements to determine the size of the lining fabric.

3. Cut lining and slip it into the box to check measurements. Determine placement of any pockets that are to be added to the lining and that will end up on the inside of the finished box. Ends of the lining fabric will be overlapped later and glued.

4. To make pockets, see page 151.

5. Apply fabric glue to one inside wall of the box. With top edge of lining fabric even with top edge of box, place lining on the glued wall, making sure that pockets line up as planned. (Avoid having a pocket occur at any corner.) Continue around inside of box.

6. When all inside walls have been glued, turn the remaining 1″ (2.5 cm) of the lining under ½″ (12 mm) and glue, overlapping onto the first wall. This should overlap about ½″ (12 mm).

7. Glue bottom 1″ (2.5 cm) of lining to box bottom, folding at corners or clipping to make lining lie flat.

8. Cut a piece of cardboard ¼″ (6 mm) smaller than the dimensions of the bottom of the box. Cover it with fabric, overlapping edges about 1″

144 (2.5 cm). Insert this in the box to be sure of proper fit. This bottom can be glued permanently in place or left loose so it can be removed for cleaning.

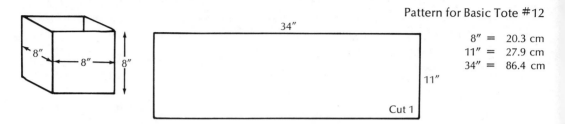

Pattern for Basic Tote #12

34"

11"

Cut 1

8" = 20.3 cm
11" = 27.9 cm
34" = 86.4 cm

8" 8" 8"

TO COVER THE OUTSIDE OF BOX:

1. Measure outside of box and add 3" (7.6 cm) to height and 2" (5.1 cm) to the length. This gives the dimensions for the cut rectangle of fabric as shown in the pattern.
2. Cut material and turn the top edge under ¼" (6 mm). Topstitch.
3. One inch (2.5 cm) away from one corner, apply glue to large portion of box wall and position cover fabric with the end of the fabric parallel to the corner wall. Leave ¾" (18 mm) of fabric extending above box top, and the rest of the excess fabric at bottom of box.
4. Continue gluing fabric around box.
5. Bring the end of the fabric to where cover fabric started, turn raw edge over ½" (12 mm), and overlap. Glue turned edge.
6. Apply glue to the top edge of the inside box. It should cover an area ½" (12 mm) wide, or wide enough to glue all of the overlapping fabric.
7. Fold cover fabric to inside of box, easing corner, and press onto the glue.
8. Turn box upside down. Fold fabric over box bottom as for wrapping a package. Cut away excess fabric at corners to make fabric lie flat.

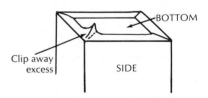

BOTTOM

Clip away excess

SIDE

9. To finish the bottom of the box, cut a piece of fabric the same size as the bottom of the box. Turn under ½" (12 mm) all around, topstitch, and glue to bottom of box. Or use naugahyde, vinyl, oilcloth, felt, or any fabric-backed material. Cut ½" (12 mm) smaller than box bottom, then glue in place.

Box tote with naugahyde handles.

TO ADD HANDLES:

1. Cut 2 handles 3″ (7.6 cm) by 44″ (111.8 cm) and sew as for turned handles. Join the ends so they will go around the box.
2. Center the seam where the handles are joined on the bottom of the box and glue handles to the bottom. Glue or tack the handles to the top edge of the box.

VARIATION — DRAWSTRING TOTE OVER BOX

1. Choose box and line inside as in directions for basic pattern. Add 1″ (2.5 cm) to top edge so that the fabric folds over top edge of box.
2. Measure outside of box and add 1″ 2.5 cm) to the distance around it. Find height of box and add the number of inches you wish to make the drawstring top. When finished height of the tote is determined, add another 2″ (5.1 cm) to allow for a folded hem at top to make drawstring channel.
3. See Basic Tote #6 (page 131) for drawstring top directions.
4. Sew sides to form a tube.
5. Slip tube over box with 2″ (5.1 cm) of extra fabric extending below bottom of box for gluing.
6. Finish by gluing bottom 2″ (5.1 cm) of fabric to bottom of box as described in basic pattern. The outside walls of the box are not glued to the fabric; only the bottom is glued.
7. Cut a piece of any nonwoven material ½″ (12 mm) smaller on all sides than bottom of box. Glue to cover box bottom and the raw edges of fabric.
8. Insert drawstring.

15. Finishing

Much of the final design character of any tote results from the details of finishing. A contrasting color for binding adds crisp trim, or a patterned lining gives a surprise of color. The simplest bag may take on a smart tailored look through the addition of metal rings or a leather strap. Following are directions for the various finishing techniques: handles, pockets, binding, grommeting, lettering and graphics, and decorating.

HANDLES

Making Self-Fabric Handles

TURNED HANDLES Cut fabric according to basic tote pattern, which includes a ½″ (12-mm) seam allowance. For lightweight fabrics, or for handles of at least 1½″ (3.8 cm) in width, fold material lengthwise with right sides facing. Join long edges of one handle and turn. This forms a long, tube-like shape. Press with seam at center back. When tube has been pressed, tuck ends of the tubes inside themselves and slip-stitch the end shut. This provides a finished end for the handle. The handles can then be left as is, or they can be top-stitched for extra firmness.

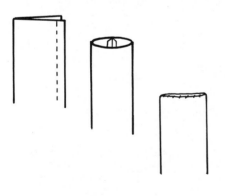

Turning is not suitable for heavy materials or for narrow handles because of the difficulty in turning the tube right side out. Shiny vinyl is extremely difficult to turn because of its tendency to stick to itself.

STITCHED HANDLES For heavier fabrics, vinyls, and for narrow handles, fold under the seam allowances on the long edges and press. Fold the handle

lengthwise so that pressed edges meet. Baste and topstitch the open side,
then sew a matching line of top stitching on the other side. If ends of handles
have to be finished, tuck handle ends in
before topstitching. When handles go on
the outside of a tote, the ends should be
finished by turning under before stitching. When they are attached inside a
tote, finishing is optional.

LINED HANDLES   To have a contrasting color on the underside of handles,
cut each handle the width of the finished handle plus ½″ (12-mm) seam allowance on each side. Cut identical handles for facing. Turn under ½″
(12-mm) on each long edge and press. Place handle with lining, wrong
sides together and pressed edges meeting. Pin and baste. Then topstitch. If
ends of handles should be finished, tuck handle ends in before stitching.

Attaching Handles

Once handles are made, they can be attached to the tote in any of several ways. If the tote has a seam line at the top edge, the handle or strap can
be inserted and caught in place when the seam is sewn.

When straps wrap all the way around a tote (see page 150), they should
be sewn to flat fabric before the tote parts are assembled. Topstitch at each
edge of strap and reinforce at top edge of tote.

To attach handles outside of the
tote, the ends must be finished. Then use
an attaching stitch that runs parallel to
top stitching on tote, or use a reinforced
stitch. Both of these are shown in the
drawing.

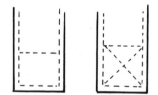

ATTACHING INSIDE   Pin handles to
inside of bag with handle ends overlapping the top stitching or top hemline.
These inside handles may be secured in
either of two ways. If they are pinned in
place before the open end of the bag is
topstitched, 1 line of sewing will accomplish both steps and the handles are
caught in with the topstitched line. The

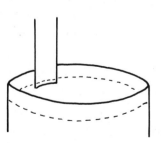

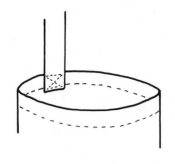

148   finished ends of the handles are then slip-stitched in place. If the tote has already been topstitched, the handles are pinned and basted in place and then further top stitching will be needed. The drawing shows two sewing methods to accomplish this.

ATTACHING OUTSIDE Pin finished ends of handles to the outside of the finished tote bag. The end of the handle should overlap the line of top stitching at the open end of the tote. Baste, then topstitch handle in place using parallel or reinforced stitches as shown in the drawing. An outside attachment that forms a decorative loop is shown in the second drawing. Metal rings or other finishing details can be slipped onto these loops before they are stitched.

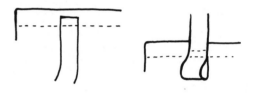

Ready-made Handles

Some ready-made straps are available in nylon or cotton. These have finished edges and are exceptionally durable and strong. The heavier woven bands are available at awning companies, upholsterers' shops, tent or mountaineering suppliers, and at some hardware stores. Lighter weight straps are often available at notions counters.

A lightweight bag can easily be carried by grosgrain ribbon or other decorative woven-edging handles. Strips of leather can be used and are especially attractive on natural-colored fabrics. Be sure to use a specially made leather needle in your sewing machine for stitching leather.

Rope handles add a sporty and rugged look. Ends can be run through grommet openings, then knotted to keep them in place. A ½" (12-mm) rope is comfortable to hold, though smaller or larger diameter rope is also appropriate. Colored nylon ropes are attractive, though the ends must be melted to keep them from raveling. Some stores that sell synthetic ropes (boat shops, particularly) have a device that does this for you, so know your measurements when you purchase your rope.

Drawstring Ties

For drawstrings that match a tote, tubing can be made from a long, narrow strip of fabric. This sometimes gets very difficult to turn, however, and it is unquestionably easier to use a ready-made drawstring.

Cotton corded tubing is available in almost all notions departments. Velvet tubing adds an elegant touch, while cotton cording is an inexpensive and attractive solution.

Leather thongs, satin ribbons, grosgrain ribbons, and military braid all offer a variety of colors and textures for drawstrings. For tiny bags, use yarn, string, or narrow ribbons which add colorful touches.

Handle Placement

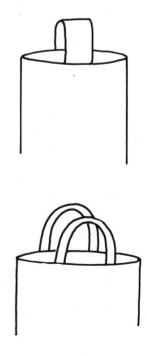

SINGLE HANDLE ACROSS CENTER   Attach handle to inside or outside of bag at center top edge. The handle should be long enough to allow easy access to tote.

DOUBLE HANDLE ATTACHED SAME SIDE Make 2 handles of the same length and width. Attach each one to one side of the tote, so that the top is free from any handles crossing it. Adjust placement of handles on sides to the size and weight of the tote. If handles are too widely spaced, the bag cannot be carried easily without buckling. The space between the two ends of a handle may vary from about 2½″ (6.4 cm) to 8″ (21 cm). Pin the handles in place experimentally to determine the best placement.

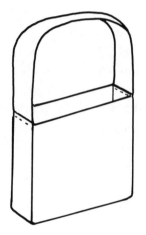

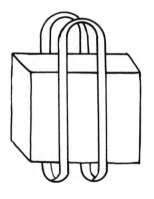

DOUBLE HANDLES ATTACHED TO OPPOSITE SIDES Make 2 handles of the same length and width. Attach one end to each side across the opening. Experiment and adjust placement to size and weight of bag. This way of attaching handles does not give easy access to the contents of tote unless the handles are fairly long.

SINGLE HANDLE FROM ENDS This handle is most often used on totes with side panels or insets. It is not a practical handle for flat bags. Make the handle the desired length for arm or over-the-shoulder use. Finish ends and sew handle to either the inside or the outside. In some patterns the side panels are continuous with the handle, being cut from 1 long piece.

For flat bags, a single handle used at the ends must be narrow. Spaghetti strap, cording, or narrow ribbon or braid will work well.

CONTINUOUS HANDLE UNDER BAG When extra strength is required from the handles, as when a tote is expected to carry a heavy weight, it will be helpful to have handles that go all the way under the tote. One continuous strap can be used. This will be more easily applied before the tote parts are assembled and it must be topstitched. Placement will vary according to the specific tote.

Handle Lengths

Lengths for handles will vary greatly and are often a matter of personal preference. A person's height will affect the desired length for a shoulder strap, for example. And the length of the bag itself will affect the length of the handle needed. However, as a general guide, here are some more or less standard handle lengths (finished size from top of tote):

Briefcase type tote: 7″ (17.8 cm)
Over arm tote: 10″ to 15″ (25.4 cm to 38.1 cm)
Short over-the-shoulder: 22″ (55.9 cm)
Long over-the-shoulder: 33″ to 40″ (83.8 cm to 101.6 cm)
Over head and shoulder: 33″ to 40″ (83.8 cm to 101.6 cm)

POCKETS

Few details add more to the enjoyable use of a tote than the addition of small pockets on either the inside or the outside. Pockets are most easily added to the lining or to the tote material, before the parts are joined, while the fabric is still lying completely flat. Pockets can be made for specific purposes on various bags. For example, a shopping bag might need small pockets for car keys, house keys, bus fare, or parking meter change. A beach bag might need special pockets for sunglasses or lotion. Someone who spends time riding the subway or ferryboat would enjoy an outside pocket for a paperback book. The book pocket or magazine pocket can be made to fit any favorite publication by adding a patch pocket to the outside of the tote. The pocket should be slightly wider and shorter than the magazine so it can be easily removed. Some pockets require closures, others can be open. Most pockets are made by one of the following methods:

Patch Pocket

Cut pocket to desired size, allowing an extra ½″ (12 mm) at each edge plus an additional 1″ (2.5 cm) at the top. Turn under the ½″ (12-mm) hem allowance on all 4 edges and press. Then turn the top edge down the additional 1″ (2.5 cm) and topstitch the top edge. Pin the pocket in place, baste, and topstitch the sides and bottom to tote or lining.

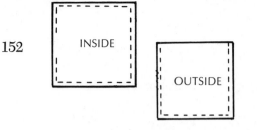

Lined Pocket

Cut 2 pockets, one for the outside and one for the lining. Place right sides together and sew, catching all 4 corners but leaving an opening on one side. Turn, press, and slip-stitch the opening shut. Either whipstitch or topstitch the pocket to the tote or the lining.

Continuous Pocket

Several pockets can be made for the inside or outside of a bag by joining 2 rectangular fabric pieces and sewing them as in lined pocket above. Topstitch to tote or lining by sewing the pocket at the sides and at bottom, then stitch divisions or compartments in the large pocket.

Zippered Pocket

Cut pocket, allowing an additional 1″ (2.5 cm) for the zipper as well as the usual ½″ (12-mm) seam allowance at

each edge. Cut the pocket into 2 pieces by cutting straight across, 2″ (5.1 cm) from the top edge. Rejoin those parts with a ½″ (12-mm) seam, leaving an opening for a short, invisible zipper. Sew zipper in place according to zipper instructions. Turn under all raw edges of pocket, press, and baste in place. Topstitch all 4 sides to tote or lining.

Concealed Zipper Pocket

Cut the lining for the tote, adding an extra 3″ (7.6 cm) to the height of the side on which the pocket will be used. Cut the material 4″ (10.2 cm) from the top as for the zippered pocket above. Insert zipper and sew as zipper package instructs, but do not topstitch it. Then fold the lining down 1″ (2.5 cm) over the zipper as in the drawing.

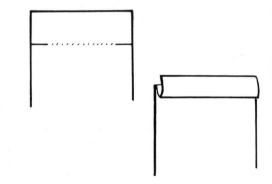

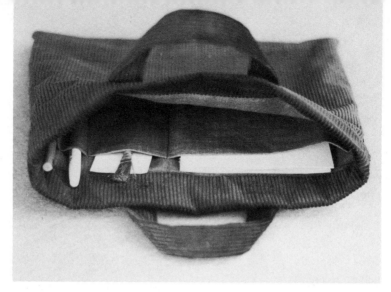

For specific uses continuous pockets can be made of various widths.

Cut a second piece of lining the same width as the one in which the zipper is sewn, and as deep as the finished pocket is to be. Machine-stitch the pocket backing to the lining, matching raw edges at top and at sides and sewing ¼″ (6 mm) from raw edge. Then proceed to assemble the lining as called for in the tote directions.

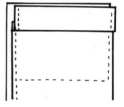

To make a small, concealed zipper pocket, insert a zipper as described above. Cut backing fabric to desired pocket size. Place backing behind zipper area and outline pocket, sewing through backing and lining as in the drawing.

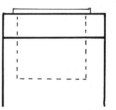

Slot Pocket

Cut lining material with an additional 1″ (2.5 cm) in the tote height. Cut lining 2″ (5.1 cm) from the top as in the zipper pocket above. Then resew with a ½″ (12-mm) seam, leaving an opening in the center. Topstitch edges of the opening, as in the drawing. Place

a rectangle of fabric behind the stitched slot. The slot can be of any size, up to the full width of the lining, as long as there is 1″ (2.5 cm) of stitched seam at each side. The rectangle can be the full size of the lining or it can be a smaller pocket shape within the edges of the lining. Topstitch pocket fabric in place as in the drawing.

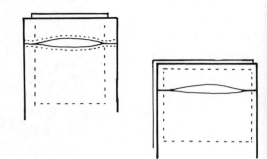

BINDING

This is a simple, colorful method of finishing. When heavy fabrics, such as canvas or duck are used, raw edges can be bound rather than hemmed or lined. Seams and edges of handles or straps can be finished with binding.

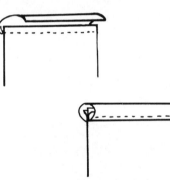

Bias strips can be cut either from matching or contrasting fabric. Lighter weight materials will be easier to work with. Bias strips are sewn to the raw edge of the tote fabric, right sides facing. The bias is then folded over the raw edge, turned under, pressed, and hand-stitched on the back as in the drawing. This works well on quilted fabrics or other heavy but soft materials.

The process can be reversed so that the bias is sewn to the wrong side of the fabric, drawn over the raw edge, turned under, and topstitched on the right side. On very heavy fabrics this method is simpler.

Binding is much more easily accomplished if a ready-made binding is used. Bias tape is among the most inexpensive and readily available. The edges of bias tape are already folded which simplifies the sewing process. Woven bias edgings are also available at most fabric shops and notions departments. These are heavier and come in a limited range of colors. Since they have finished edges, no hemming is required.

On some totes the easiest method of finishing the top open edge will be to use binding. Trim fabrics so that raw edges of tote and lining are even. Baste, then stitch binding.

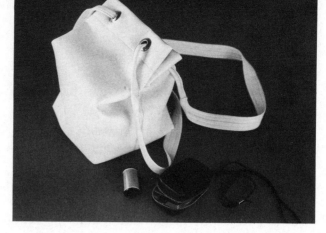

Grommeting is a tidy way
to attach straps.

GROMMETING

Grommeting is an attractive means of reinforcing holes cut in fabric. By encircling the hole with the metal ring, the material is protected so that cord or rope can be run through it for handles or for a drawstring top.

Fabric shops and notions departments carry a variety of grommets. Some are square but most are circular. All grommets consist of two metal rings which clamp together over the cloth. The metal opening in the center is for the thong, cord, or rope. Grommets are especially functional on duffels, canvas bags, or drawstring bags.

A three-part tool is sold with the grommets. One part cuts a hole in the fabric, another holds the bottom grommet in place, and the third is placed over the top of the upper grommet and through the hole. A hammer is used to pound the two pieces of metal together. Complete directions are given with the grommet tool and parts. If the fabric is lightweight or thin, the grommet tool does not cut through it easily. It may be necessary to cut the hole with a pair of small scissors. Practice on extra material before jabbing holes into your beautiful new tote!

LETTERING AND GRAPHICS

Nothing personalizes a tote so definitely as lettering, whether a monogram, a name, or words are used. Children's bags and travel totes almost require this type of identification. The following are suggestions for some simplified methods of adding simple graphics to your totes:

Stencils

Stencils provide quick, ready-made patterns for letters which can be used over and over. Precut stencils are available in a variety of heights and sizes from stationers and from dime stores or school supply stores. Plan the placement of letters by first drawing them on a piece of paper.

There are a number of permanent paints or inks that work well on fabric. Trace letters on fabric using pencil or felt-tip markers. Remove stencil and fill in the letters with marking pens, liquid embroidery, or fabric crayons. If you wish a color lighter than the fabric, inks and dyes are difficult to use as the background color shows through the dye color. For white or light letters, use acrylic paint applied with a stiff bristle brush. Regular stencil paint is also available in art supply stores. Most of these paints and inks are permanent. Lettering applied from marking pens and similar dyes is often made more permanent when ironed with a hot iron as it sometimes helps set the color. Iron from the reverse side. Test ink or paint on the particular fabric you are using, since different fibers absorb the colors in different ways.

Iron-on Fabric

One of the most direct ways to add letters and graphics to totes is to use iron-on tape. The iron-on fabric, which has the advantage of speed, is sold as bonding tape, mending tape, or iron-on tape or fabric. Packages of patches or strips are available in department stores, dime stores, or fabric shops. Cut the letters or other designs and iron them on the fabric before the tote pieces are assembled. The fabric adheres best when there is a smooth surface over which to work, and seams can interfere with the fusing of the fabric. Follow the directions that accompany the package of iron-on fabric.

Bonding Fabrics

Another method of adding letters or graphics, similar to that of iron-on fabric, is the use of a sheet of bonding material. It requires heat to set and will fuse two pieces of material together. The layer of bonding material is placed between the tote fabric and the material to which it is to be applied. The advantage of this method is that you can use your own lightweight fabric for lettering or designs. The only disadvantage is that the letters and the bonding fabric must be cut identically and carefully positioned before being heat-set. Cut the letters or graphics first, then use them as patterns for cutting the bonding material. When placing the two layers on the tote fabric, be sure that there is no bonding material exposed at the edges of the letters. With bonding materials you can use letters or cutouts of any size. Be sure to obtain material that fuses two fabrics together— not a one-way bonding fabric like an iron-on interfacing.

Machine Appliqué

Cut designs or letters from fabric and place them on the unassembled, flat pieces of your tote. Baste to tote fabric. A straight stitch around the letters leaves the raw edge of fabric exposed which gives a frayed or soft look. This is especially nice with a denim. A machine satin stitch binds the edge and adds a solid line of color which can be a strong decorative element in the design.

DECORATING

Totes are marvelous recipients of talents of every sort. Whether your forte is batik, stencil, tie-dye, quilting, or embroidery, your tote stands ready to receive, use, and display it. Decorative additions are most easily handled by sewing the finished, designed fabric to a cut piece of the tote. Then the tote is assembled. Or the tote parts can be cut, the embellishments added to those parts, and then the parts assembled. It is always more cumbersome and confining to try to add details to an already-made tote than to treat the flat fabric.

Printed cotton flower petals with raised centers by Karen Bray.

Totes Made from the Twelve Basic Totes

Basic Tote #1 (Side Inset Tote)

All-day bag and shaving kit, 68
Bag it, 62
Bike backpack, 78
Black and white book tote, 32
Gardener's tote, 51
Patchwork poke, 20

Sewing tote, 84
Tamelin's stuff, 38
Teacher's tote, 30
Tennis tote, 89
Travel set, 66
Traveling coffee tote, 61

Basic Tote #2 (One-Piece Boxed Tote)

Artist's carryall, 34
Bev's tote, 55
Blue denim 24-hour tote, 32
Camera tote, 97
Flower tote, 20
Giant office tote, 26
Giant striped tote, 18
Lunch tote, 59

Office tote, 36
Onion bag, 17
Quilted tennis tote, 88
Sleeping bag totes, 102
Striped rain tote, 76
Trapunto landscape tote, 22
The way to my heart, 58

Basic Tote #3 (Envelope Bag)

Backpack, 74
Cyclist's tote, 72
Denim evening bag, 111
Designer's tote, 26

Mylar makeup tote, 106
Rain tote, 78
Silk evening bag, 105
Tote-it-along, 33

Basic Tote #4 (Boxed Bag)

Bird-watcher's bag, 97
Doll shoulder bag, 46
Elephantote, 119
Executive's bag, 35
Place mat tote, 54
Scenic shopping tote, 15

Security bag, 120
Shopper's tote, 16
Shoulder bag, 118
Sunburst bag, 25
Window tote, 37

Basic Tote #5 (Flat Tote)

Biker's bag, 95

Canvas tote, 28

Denim heart bag, 23

Doggy bag, 112

Monogrammed bag, 29

Onion bag, 17

Patchwork face bag, 108

Rat pak, 43

Sewing pocket, 82

Shoe bag, 81

Woman's bag, 116

Basic Tote #6 (Drawstring Tote)

Gift bags, 53

His and hers totes, 91

Jewelry tote, 75

Kid's carryall, 42

Runaway totes, 73

Stocking cap tote, 42

To the beach, 95

Velveteen evening bag, 108

Basic Tote #7 (Cylinders)

Lesson tote, 40

Oatmeal box tote, 40

Padded sewing tote, 85

Picnic tote, 56

Rainbow lunch bag, 61

Recycled denim tote, 63

Swim and gym tote, 92

Basic Tote #8 (Three-Piece Shoulder Tote)

Silk three-piece tote, 35

Stars and stripes, 18

Tree bag, 23

Basic Tote #9 (Triangular Tie Tote)

Striped tie tote, 24

Walrus tote, 45

Woven jute tote, 117

Basic Tote #10 (One-Piece Tote)

Hobo tote, 55

Scarf tote, 17

Toy tote, 44

Zippered gardener's tote, 49

Basic Tote #11 (Roll-up Tote)

Ms.'s tool kit, 53

Pill tote, 70

Travel roll-up tote, 66

Basic Tote #12 (Covered Box Tote)

Garden tote, 50

Plaid picnic tote, 56

Sport tote, 93

There are a few totes in this book which are not made on the basic tote patterns, but which have individual patterns of their own. We have always given the pattern for these totes in the text.

And the totes in Chapter 13, "A Gallery of Unusual Totes," have no patterns as they are the work of various fiber artists and craftspeople and were included here to stimulate your creativeness. Many of them are built on the basic totes and when they are we have made a note of it.